JENN, ♡

   I HOPE YOU ENJOY THE BOOK!
CAN'T WAIT TO HEAR ABOUT
YOUR COOKING ADVENTURES!

           —Christy

May the course be with you!

           — Charles

THE NICE GUYS GUIDE TO COOKING FOR A LADY

THE NICE GUYS GUIDE TO COOKING FOR A LADY

CHRISTY BEAVER
&
CHARLES LIOTTA

ISBN-10: 1519669763
ISBN-13: 978- 1519669766

FORWARD

• •

The Nice Guy's Guide To Cooking For a Lady flambéed into existence when Christy Beaver (The Beav) made a present for her hapless single dude-friend Charles Liotta (The Chuckman). Charles, terrified of women in general, told The Beav a specific fear around not knowing how to cook a meal "with ingredients and stuff" fit for serving a female companion should he ever have a chance to host one in his home. More specifically, he explained that to him a 'meal' was a sleeve of stackable snack chips. The Chuckman was resigned to his inevitable fate of lonely solitude and prepackaged meals when suddenly, The Beav surprised him with a gift tailored to his culinarily-challenged needs. At the time the title for the book was "Chuckman's Recipes To Impress the Ladies." (Subsequent working titles included "The Seduction Reduction," "The Little Black Cookbook," and "Everything You've Ever Wanted to Know About Cooking, but Were Afraid to Ask.")

Eventually His Chuckness began attempting to cook some of the delicacies documented in the veritable tome. As much fun as it was to pursue this epic endeavor, it became more and more apparent with each attempt that there was a significant disconnect between the knowledge and vernacular of a young lady who grew up cooking, and any man...ever. Each meal resulted in numerous panicked phone calls to The Beav inquiring about a range of questions from "what the heck is a 'leek?'" to "how thick is 'sliced?'" Several things became clear: 1) Everyone NEEDS access a book like this! 2) Every nice guy should to be able to call The Beav each time they cook. (Instead we went with providing Advice From a Real Live Girl section since Christy had some curious reservations about giving out her phone #.) 3) If men are going to use it, it's got to be as brief as possible and only require readily available ingredients. 4) Lots of photos so men don't have to read. 5) There 'needs' to be a lot of puns. 6) There should be a place in the back to store takeout menus in case all goes poorly. 7) Every recipe should end with "All that's left is for *someone* to kiss the cook." You're welcome.

After a lot of work to compost excess words, complexities, and jargon, while maximizing useful photos, hilarity, and deliciousness, we offer for your consideration The Nice Guy's Guide to Cooking For a Lady. Because everyone has a quality fellow in their life who could use a little help feeling confident entertaining someone he cares about. We sincerely hope that this resource will help nice guys everywhere feel comfortable hosting a meal that anyone would thoroughly appreciate and enjoy. We here at The Nice Guy's Guide To Cooking For a Lady firmly believe that the only thing a nice guy should finish last is dessert.

CORNUCOPIA • OF • CONTENTS

MANSLATIONS

Measurement	Also Known As
1 Gallon	4 Quarts
1 Quart	0.91635295 Liter
1 Liter	4 Cups(ish)
1 Cup	8 Oz
1 Oz	2 Tbsp
1 Tbsp	3 Tsp
1 Tsp	5 ml
1 ml	barely anything
Chopped	Diced + a little
Diced	Minced + a little
Minced	Sliced + a little
Sliced	Really tiny
Shredded	Grated + a little
Grated	Shredded - some

Manslation
The amount of milk
Size of a bottle of motor oil
Think moonshine bought in a jar
A baseball minus a golf ball worth
1/12th of a beer (bottle/can)
A pirate's eye patch worth
A baseball player's lip-chew bulge
Don't even worry about it
Sawdust from a rusty chain saw
Sawdust from a sharp chain saw
Fish tank little blue pebble sized
Stuff stuck in your teeth after eating
Make the food minnow sized
Powderified

DATE CHECKLIST

Photocopy and complete the page to the right for each
lady you cook for.

HINT: For the love of all that is holy, if she divulges any
of this information make sure to get what she wants, avoid
what she does not, and satisfy her needs! You know all
those words they're always saying, they're paying attention
to if you're paying attention to them or not. It's a test, if
you learn nothing else at all from this book learn THAT, and
it will be a small price to pay for such critical insight.

Do you have any allergies?
(Because accidentally poisoning her might put a real damper on your relationship)

☐ (Check box if none), otherwise list allergies (and avoid them):

_____

Do you have any dietary restrictions or foods you avoid?
☐ Vegan?   (No animal products)
☐ Vegetarian?   (No meat)
☐ Pescatarian?   (Seafood okay, no other meats)
☐ Paleo?   (Dinosaur diet)
☐ Whole food?   (Nothing processed)
☐ Cilantro?   (To some people it tastes like soap, ask her before including it!)
☐ Other: _____

What is your favorite beverage to drink with meals?
☐ Wine
    ☐ Red: Syrah (or Shiraz), Merlot, Cabernet Sauvignon, Malbec, Pinot Noir, Zinfandel, Sangiovese, Barbera
        Other: _____
        Brand: _____
    ☐ White: Chardonnay, Pinot Grigio / Pinot Gris, Chenin Blanc, Gerwurztraminer, Sauvignon Blanc, Semillon, Viognier
        Other: _____
        Brand: _____
☐ Beer: Amber, Bitter, Blonde, Bock, Brown, Golden, Hefeweizen, IPA, Pale Ale, Porter, Red, Saison, Stout
    Other: _____
    Brand: _____
☐ Cider
    Other: _____
    Brand: _____
☐ Other even girlier options
    Other: _____
    Brand: _____

What is your favorite kind of chocolate?
☐ Dark (% Cacao: _____)
☐ Milk
☐ White
☐ Other: _____

Is there anything else at all you can think of I could do in advance to make our time together as comfortable and pleasant an experience for you as possible?
Her answer here: _____

CHAPTER 1

BRUNCH

Since the dawn of time man has been reluctantly opening one eye, harrumphing, and hitting the snooze button either literally or metaphorically until twilight, perhaps again at sunrise, and let's be honest continuing this process until well into the following afternoon if possible. Alas and alack mankind's folly put at risk the most basic and important reason to wake up at all - to eat bacon. Breakfast being the most bacon-intensive meal, society found itself desperately needing to evolve and invent a superior meal allowing for breakfast meats to be consumed until the afternoon. A few superfluous pieces of fruit garnish later and humanity had spewed forth perhaps the greatest innovation of all peopledom, BRUNCH; a meal that combines breakfast foods with the official kickoff of it being okay to drink alcohol for the day. So be with me now people and let us embrace, rejoice, and celebrate the greatness that is life on Brunch, for everyone knows that Breakfast is the most important meal of the day, and that Brunch is even importanter.

THERE WILL BE BLOODY MARYS

THE WORLD'S FINEST MARINADE FOR GREEN OLIVES

NOT EVERYONE KNOWS THIS, BUT I'M SO AFRAID OF COMMITMENT I WON'T EVEN TALK TO A GIRL IF SHE'S NAMED 'MARY'

2 oz vodka

3 stuffed green olives

1 tsp Worcestershire sauce

bloody mary mix

kosher salt

3 - 4 of the following optional:

    strip of bacon

    mozzarella string cheese

    cheddar string cheese

    pepperoncini

    sausage (pepperoni/salami/breakfast)

    lemon and/or lime wedge

    stick of celery

    shrimp

    jalapeno

    cherry or grape tomato

    pickled onion

- Put salt on a plate
- Dip rims of 2 pint glasses 1" into water
- Without turning glasses upright, dip rim in salt and twist
- Fill glasses halfway with ice
- Pour 2 oz vodka, bloody mary mix, and 1 tsp Worcestershire, into glasses leaving room for ingredients. Stir
- Add olives and your preference of 3 to 4 other items from the list provided
- All that's left is for *someone* to kiss the cook

ADVICE FROM A REAL LIVE GIRL:
USE TEQUILA INSTEAD OF VODKA FOR A
"BLOODY MARIA."

DIDN'T GET THE MEMO-SAS

PAIRS WELL WITH LIFE

NOT EVERYONE KNOWS THIS, BUT ORANGE JUICE COMBINED WITH CHAMPAGNE IS EFFECTIVELY LIQUID SUNSHINE

1 bottle champagne
1 orange (optional fanciness)
orange juice

•Set out two wine glasses
•Fill each one to 1" below the brim with
champagne
•Pour in ½" of juice
•Optional: Place an orange slice on the rim
•All that's left is for *someone* to kiss the cook

ADVICE FROM A REAL LIVE GIRL:
OJ IS THE TRADITIONAL OPTION HERE BUT IF YOU
CHOOSE GRAPEFRUIT, MANGO, CRANBERRY, OR
POMEGRANATE YOU LOOK VERY FANCY AND IN A
GOOD WAY.

RED-Y FOR LOVE BEER

IT'S NOON SOMEWHERE...

NOT EVERYONE KNOWS THIS BUT, "BEER:30" ISN'T SO MUCH A TIME AS A STATE OF MIND AND/OR SOBRIETY

12 oz cheap beer

tomato juice

•Set out two pint glasses
•Pour ½ of the beer into each glass
•Top with tomato juice
•All that's left is for *someone* to kiss the cook

ADVICE FROM A REAL LIVE GIRL:
THESE RED BEERS ARE ALL THE RAGE NOWADAYS.

SOUFFLEGGS

THESE GREAT EGGSPECTATIONS ARE FREQUICHELY EASY TO ACHIEVE

NOT EVERYONE KNOWS THIS, BUT THE EGG CAME LONG BEFORE THE CHICKEN. SOME DINOSAURS WERE LAYING THEM WELL OVER 65 MILLION YEARS AGO.

½ lb breakfast sausage (spicy- optional)

6 eggs

¼ cup 2% milk

2 sprigs basil

¼ cup cheddar cheese

¼ medium sized red beefsteak tomato

3 tbsp of salsa (optional)

3 tbsp of sour cream (optional)

•Fry sausage over medium heat in 12" skillet
•Break meat into ½" morsels
•Brown until no red/pink is left inside pieces
•Drain excess fat into a melting-proof vessel
•In 8" bowl combine 6 eggs and ¼ cup milk
•Beat eggs until yolk & whites become uniform
•Rinse basil, remove stems, and mince leaves
•Add egg mixture to drained sausage in skillet
•Reduce heat to lowest setting (often "simmer")
•Allow covered eggs to set up for 10 minutes
•Rinse tomato and dice into ¼" cubed pieces
•Grate the cheese
•Sprinkle cheese, basil, and tomatoes over eggs
•Do NOT stir
•Cover the pan and walk away as the eggs set up for
 an additional 10+ minutes
•Once the top of the eggs have set up to the point
 where they are no longer runny, remove from heat
 and separate into sections like a pie/pizza
•Apply a dollop of salsa and/or sour cream to taste
•All that's left is for *someone* to kiss the cook

ADVICE FROM A REAL LIVE GIRL:
THIS DISH IS LIKE THE LAZY MAN'S QUICHE. AND
QUICHE IS FANCY.

BREAKFANTASTIC BURRITO

IF SOCIETY EVER EVOLVES ANOTHER MEAL, FIRST ORDER OF BUSINESS IS TO
MAKE A BURRITO VERSION OF THAT TOO

NOT EVERYONE KNOWS THIS, BUT BREAKFAST IS ONE OF THE 5 MOST
IMPORTANT MEALS OF THE DAY

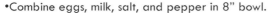

2 tortillas

4 eggs

¼ cup milk

8 oz canned black beans

1 tbsp butter

1 red pepper

2 tbsp cilantro

salt & pepper

cheddar cheese

Toppings Bar:

        salsa

        guacamole

        sour cream

- Combine eggs, milk, salt, and pepper in 8" bowl.
- Beat eggs until yolk & whites become uniform
- Grate the cheese
- Rinse cilantro, remove stems, and mince leaves
- Drain and rinse the beans
- Heat butter on medium heat in a 12" skillet
- Rinse red pepper, remove stem/seeds, chop into ¼" cubes
- When skillet is hot add peppers and ½ cup beans, cook 1 minute
- Add egg/milk mixture to the skillet and scramble
- In 5 minutes add cilantro and turn off the heat
- Microwave tortillas for 15 seconds wrapped in a paper towel
- Fill each tortilla with scrambled eggs
- Top with salsa, guacamole, sour cream, cheese
- Roll up and serve
- All that's left is for *someone* to kiss the cook

> ADVICE FROM A REAL LIVE GIRL:
> IF YOU WANT TO BE EXTRA-FANCY YOU CAN WRAP A
> FEW TORTILLAS IN FOIL AND PUT THEM IN THE OVEN ON
> "WARM" OR THE LOWEST TEMP YOUR OVEN HAS WHILE
> YOU COOK THE EGGS.

AN ELABORATE BREAKFAST SANDWICH

WE EAT MORE SANDWICHES BY BREAKFAST THAN SOME COUPLES EAT ALL DAY

NOT EVERYONE KNOWS THIS, BUT AN ELABORATE RUSE WITHOUT THE ELABORANCE IS JUST A CHEAP TRICK

2 biscuits, bagels, or English muffins

2 eggs

1 ripe avocado

breakfast meat of your choice

butter

salsa

cheese slices

•Melt butter in 12" pan over medium heat
•Once butter is melted crack both eggs into hot pan
•Cover pan for 3 minutes to trap heat
•Remove cover
•Assess if whites have gelled enough to flip safely
•If needed, continue to cook until eggs set further
•Slide spatula gently under eggs to avoid piercing
•Carefully flip eggs over so the yolks faces down
•Turn off heat
•Allow residual heat to cook eggs for 1 minute
•Salt and pepper the eggs to taste
•Slice the avocado
•Cook meat over medium heat in a 12" skillet
•Brown until no red/pink is left inside pieces
•Drain excess fat into a melting-proof vessel
•Toast the muffin or bagels
•Put two pieces of muffin or bagel on each plate
•Stack in sandwich-like form with eggs,
  meat, and cheese
•Add salsa (optional) and avocado as desired
•All that's left is for *someone* to kiss the cook

ADVICE FROM A REAL LIVE GIRL:
BISCUITS IN A CAN WORK GREAT FOR THESE
SAMMICHES. START THEM FIRST BEFORE MAKING
OTHER STUFF.

T.A.B.L.E. SANDWICHES

IF SHE SAYS "WE NEED TO TALK" ALWAYS TABLE THE DISCUSSION FOR A LATER DATE

NOT EVERYONE KNOWS THIS, BUT THE NEWS MEDIA SET UP AN ELABORATE RUSE REGARDING OUR CHOICE OF BREAD FOR THIS RECIPE; A PLOY KNOWN AS "FOCACCIA JOURNALISM"

4 slices of bread (or bagels halved)

1 ripe red beefsteak tomato

1 ripe avocado

8 strips of bacon

2 leaves of lettuce

4 eggs

mayo

- Preheat the oven to 350°F
- Fold a piece of tinfoil into accordion style peaks and valleys and fit it to your baking sheet
- Place bacon in single layers across the tinfoil
- Bake for 15 minutes
- Flip each piece of bacon individually using tongs
- Bake for an additional 15 minutes (30 total)
  See Bakin' Bacon recipe page 50 for more info
- Melt butter in an 8" pan over medium heat
- Once butter is melted crack both eggs into hot pan
- Cover pan for 3 minutes to trap heat
- Remove cover
- Assess if whites have gelled enough to flip safely
- If needed, continue to cook until eggs set further
- Slide spatula gently under eggs to avoid piercing
- Carefully flip eggs over so the yokes faces down
- Turn off heat
- Allow residual heat to cook eggs for 1 minute
- Rinse tomato, cut into ¼" slices
- Slice (or whip) the avocado for later application
- Apply a layer of mayo to each sandwich
- Stack completed ingredients in sandwich form
- All that's left is for *someone* to kiss the cook

Note: Once you bite into the egg the still slightly runny yolk should spill forth in delicious moistness, that's okay, in fact it's amazing

ADVICE FROM A REAL LIVE GIRL:
THE EGG WILL DRIP. BE SURE TO HAVE A NAPKIN
AVAILABLE FOR HER TO PROTECT HER DATE OUTFIT.

FRENCH KISSIN' TOAST

BECAUSE, TRAGICALLY, EVERY BREAKFAST CANNOT HAVE POWDERED SUGAR ON IT IT. THANKFULLY THIS ONE DOES.

NOT EVERYONE KNOWS THIS, BUT FRENCH TOAST DID NOT ACTUALLY ORIGINATE IN FRANCE, WHICH IS KIND OF CRÊPE-Y IF YOU ASK ME

4 slices of bread

3 eggs

¼ cup milk

½ tsp cinnamon

1 tbsp butter

1 tbsp powdered sugar

maple syrup

sliced strawberries

blueberries

- Combine eggs, milk, and cinnamon in a 6" bowl
- Beat eggs until yolk and whites become uniform
- Put butter in 12" skillet over medium heat to melt
- Dip each piece of bread in egg mixture to coat
- Cook in skillet on both sides until lightly browned (About 2 minutes on each side)
- Place French Toast on plates and sprinkle on a thin frosting of powdered sugar
- Serve with syrup and a side of strawberries and blueberries (rinsed)
- All that's left is for *someone* to kiss the cook

ADVICE FROM A REAL LIVE GIRL:
THIS TOAST IS CRAZY GOOD IF YOU USE CINNAMON
RAISIN BREAD. BUT NORMAL WHITE BREAD IS FINE
TOO.

I LOVE YUEBERRY PANCAKES

WOO HER WITH CARBS

NOT EVERYONE KNOWS THIS, BUT WITH PRACTICE, SKILL, AND DETERMINATION ONE CAN ENDEAVOR TO MAKE A SMILEY-FACE OUT OF THE BLUEBERRIES IN THE PANCAKE

1 box pancake mix
1 tsp vanilla extract
½ cup blueberries
¼ tsp cinnamon
eggs (maybe if the box requires it)
milk (maybe if the box requires it)
1 tbsp butter
maple syrup

•Follow directions on box to make pancake batter
•Add cinnamon, vanilla, and blueberries to batter
•Melt 1 tbsp butter in 12" skillet
•Scoop out batter 1/4" at a time and pour to make 3" puddles in skillet
•Cook for 4 minutes, or until little bubbles come up
•Flip and cook an additional 2 minutes until browned
•Serve with more butter and syrup
•All that's left is for *someone* to kiss the cook

ADVICE FROM A REAL LIVE GIRL:
ON THE PANCAKE MIX BOX, IT PROBABLY SAYS
SOMETHING LIKE "MAKES 27 PANCAKES". IT'S
WRONG. IT'LL MAKE LIKE 6 PANCAKES.

YOU GO, GURT

YOU'LL HAVE HER BELIEVING THIS KIND OF DELICIOUSNESS IS PARFAIT FOR THE COURSE

NOT EVERYONE KNOWS THIS, BUT JOKES ABOUT PARFAITS TEND TO WORK ON A LOT OF LAYERS

2 cups plain yogurt

1 cup fancy granola

1 banana

1 cup of berries

•In two 6" serving bowls, place 1 cup yogurt each

•Sprinkle ½ cup granola over each bowl

•Slice half banana into ¼" rounds over each bowl

•Pour ½ cup of berries evenly over both parfaits

•All that's left is for *someone* to kiss the cook

ADVICE FROM A REAL LIVE GIRL:
THIS BREAKFAST IS SIMPLE, HEALTHY, AND
AMAZINGLY IMPRESSIVE. USE IT.

LET'S NOT REHASH BROWNS

PERFECT FOR THE MORNING AFTER THE NIGHT BEFORE #HASHBROWNS

NOT EVERYONE KNOWS THIS, BUT THE FIRST HASH BROWN CAME INTO
EXISTENCE WHEN A MAN TRIED TO JUST WARM UP A REGULAR POTATO
ON THE STOVE, FAILED EPICALLY,
BUT PLAYED IT OFF EXPERTLY

2 potatoes

½ cup diced white onion

2 tbsp olive oil

1 tsp all-purpose seasoning of your choice

•Rinse potatoes, grate with cheese grater
•Place grated potatoes on a paper towel
•Place an additional paper towel on top and
 press (To drain the liquid out of the potatoes)
•Mix potatoes and onion in a big bowl
•Heat oil and half of the seasoning in 12" skillet
•Add potatoes in single layer to cook until
 browned
•Sprinkle remaining spices on top, flip and brown
•Takes long as 8 - 10 minutes on each side
•All that's left is for *someone* to kiss the cook

ADVICE FROM A REAL LIVE GIRL:
I KNOW IT'S TEMPTING, BUT ONLY FLIP THESE ONCE.
WAIT UNTIL THEY GET GOOD AND BROWN THEN FLIP.

MAD SKILLZIT SPUDS

GIRLS ONLY WANT BOYFRIENDS WHO HAVE GREAT SKILLETS

NOT EVERYONE KNOWS THIS, BUT CURIOUSLY ABSENT FROM A CERTAIN POPULAR ROLE PLAYING GAME'S LIST OF SKILLS IS THE MOST IMPORTANT SKILL OF ALL...COOKIN' FOR THE LADIES

2 potatoes

1 tsp all-purpose seasoning

2 tbsp olive oil

•Rinse potatoes, dice into approximately ½" cubes
•Heat olive oil and seasoning in a 12" skillet
•Add potatoes in a single layer
•Cook until browned, stirring occasionally for about 25 minutes
•Put a paper towel on a plate
•Place potatoes on paper towel
•Serve with ketchup or Don't Curry, Be Happy
•All that's left is for *someone* to kiss the cook

ADVICE FROM A REAL LIVE GIRL:
YOU CAN COVER THE SKILLET WITH A SHEET OF FOIL
SO THE POTATOES COOK FASTER.

SUNNY FRIED UP

WHAT CAME FIRST, DAWN OR DUSK?

NOT EVERYONE KNOWS THIS, BUT WHEN EGG WHITES DO SOMETHING WRONG THE BLAME ALWAYS FALLS ON THEIR OLDER BROTHER, IT'S A HEAVY YOKE TO BEAR.

2 eggs

1 tbsp butter

•Melt butter in an 8" pan over medium heat
•Once butter is melted crack both eggs into hot pan
•Cover pan for 3 minutes to trap heat
•Remove cover
•Assess if yolk has gelled to your ideal preference
•Appropriate setting is a matter of taste
•If needed, continue to cook until ideal for you/ her
•Slide onto serving plate
•All that's left is for *someone* to kiss the cook

ADVICE FROM A REAL LIVE GIRL:
KEEP EGGS IN THE FRIDGE. ALWAYS.

SUNNY FRIED DOWN

SHOW HER YOU'RE DOWN WITH HER SUNNY DISPOSITION

2 eggs
1 tbsp butter

•Melt butter in an 8" pan over medium heat
•Once butter is melted crack both eggs into hot pan
•Cover pan for 3 minutes to trap heat
•Remove cover
•Assess if whites have gelled enough to flip safely
•If needed, continue to cook until eggs set further
•Slide spatula gently under eggs to avoid piercing
•Carefully flip eggs over so the yolks face down
•Turn off heat
•Allow residual heat to cook eggs for 1 minute
•Slide completed eggs onto serving plate
•All that's left is for *someone* to kiss the cook

ADVICE FROM A REAL LIVE GIRL:
ASK HOW SHE LIKES HER EGGS.

LESCAMBRD GEGS

THERE SEEMS TO HAVE BEEN SOME SORT OF MIX UP...

NOT EVERYONE KNOWS THIS, BUT SCRAMBLED EGGS ARE THE MOST COMMON RESULT OF FAILED-ATTEMPTED-SUNNY-SIDE-UP EGGS

4 eggs
1 tbsp butter
¼ cup milk

•Melt butter in an 8" pan over medium heat
•Once butter is melted crack eggs into hot pan
•After 1 minute gently stir with a rubber spatula
•Push the firming eggs from pan's bottom to edges
•Continue to stir slowly every 30 seconds
•Once eggs near scrambled status turn off heat
•Salt & pepper to taste
•Allow residual heat to cook eggs for 1 minute
•Slide completed eggs onto serving plate
•All that's left is for *someone* to kiss the cook

ADVICE FROM A REAL LIVE GIRL:
FOR BONUS POINTS, ADD ¼ CUP OF
SHREDDED CHEDDAR CHEESE.

EGGS BENANICEGUY

IF YOU'VE BEEN A NICE GUY, HOW ELSE IS SHE GOING TO KNOW?

NOT EVERYONE KNOWS THIS, BUT HOLLANDAISE SAUCE IS IN NO WAY A REFERENCE TO HOLLAND'S LIBERAL DRUG POLICY

2 English muffins
1 jar of hollandaise sauce
6 strips of bacon
2 eggs
1 tablespoon butter

•Preheat 12" skillet over medium-low heat
•Cook bacon on medium-low until done, flipping once and remove from skillet
(See page 51 for an alternate way to cook bacon)
•Add butter to skillet and melt
•Add eggs and cook 2-3 minutes, and flip when whites are cooked
•Cook eggs one more minute. Turn off heat
•Toast English muffins
•Assemble ingredients into sandwich form
•Heat up the hollandaise sauce in an 8" pot over medium heat
•Pour over sandwiches
•All that's left is for *someone* to kiss the cook

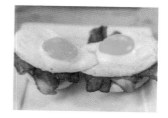

ADVICE FROM A REAL LIVE GIRL:
YOU CAN ALSO USE A DRY PACKET OF HOLLANDAISE SAUCE MIX, JUST BE SURE TO GRAB THE EXTRA INGREDIENTS WRITTEN ON THE PACKET. LIKELY MILK AND BUTTER.

PIGS IN A BLANKET, UNCOVERED

BUY LINKS OR PATTIES PRE-FORMED; YOU DON'T HAVE TO REINVENT THE SQUEAL

NOT EVERYONE KNOWS THIS, BUT PIGS EAT GARBAGE AND TURN IT INTO BACON; SUPERHEROES ARE REAL MY FRIEND, AND THEY'RE DELICIOUS!

sausage patties or links

Note: flattening patties further allows for quicker cooking

•Preheat 12" skillet over medium-low heat
•Add sausage or links to skillet
•Cook for 12-14 minutes
•Turn frequently for even browning
•Confirm there is no pink/red left inside pieces
•Drain excess fat into melt-proof vessel
•All that's left is for *someone* to kiss the cook

BAKIN' BACON

NOT EVERYONE KNOWS THIS, BUT IF SHE DOESN'T LIKE BACON IT'S
CONSIDERED A WHITE MEAT RED FLAG

1 package of bacon
Roll of tin foil

•Preheat the oven to 350°F
•Fold a piece of tinfoil into accordion style peaks
  and valleys and fit it to your baking sheet
          •The cooking bacon will drip, needs sides
•Place bacon in single layers across the tinfoil
•Bake for 20 minutes
•Flip each piece of bacon individually using
  tongs
•Bake for an additional 20-25 minutes (45 total)
•Place a paper towel on a plate
•Use tongs to place bacon on paper towel
•Allow to cool while paper towel absorbs excess
  fat
•Carefully fold tinfoil inward to contain drippings
          •Allow fat to cool/congeal then dispose
•All that's left is for *someone* to kiss the cook

ADVICE FROM A REAL LIVE GIRL:
TURKEY BACON ONLY TAKES 30 MINUTES. THAT'S
LESS TIME THAN PORK BACON.

MOMMA BEAVER'S
SOUTHERN BREAKFAST CASSEROLE

"CASSEROLE TIDE"

NOT EVERYONE KNOWS THIS, BUT THIS RECIPE IS THE BEST WAY TO 'HAVE FUN STORMING THE CASSEROLE'

6 slices of white bread	6 eggs
1 lb breakfast sausage	½ tsp salt
1 red pepper	½ tsp pepper
1 cup cheddar cheese	2 tsp Rosemary (optional)

- Preheat oven to 350°F
- Cook sausage over medium heat in 12" skillet
- Break meat into ½" morsels
- Brown until no red/pink is left inside pieces
- Chop the slices of bread into ¼" cubes
- Rinse red pepper, remove stem/seeds, chop into ¼" cubes
- Grate cheddar cheese
- Combine bread, sausage, pepper, & cheese in a 12" bowl
- Combine eggs, salt, pepper, and Rosemary in 8" bowl
- Beat eggs until yolk & whites become uniform
- Pour eggs over bread in 12" bowl, stir to coat/combine
- Spray a 4 quart (15" L x 10" W x 2" H) oven safe baking dish with cooking spray
- Put the combined bread and egg mixture in the baking dish and cover with foil
- Place baking dish in preheated oven
- Bake 45 minutes until eggs cooked and bread crisp
- Allow casserole to cool for 5-10 minutes. Enough time for a Mimosa!
- All that's left is for *someone* to kiss the cook

ADVICE FROM A REAL LIVE GIRL:
THIS DISH IS BEST IF ASSEMBLED THE NIGHT BEFORE AND EFFORTLESSLY POPPED INTO THE OVEN THE NEXT MORNING. LET THE DISH SIT OUT 15 MINUTES BEFORE BAKING TO GET TO ROOM TEMP.

SNACKHACKS

BRUNCH EDITION

Some food components, or "snacks" if you will, are so literally self-explanatory (the directions are simple and right on the box) that they don't warrant a recipe; however, it's a useful resource to have a list of options/ideas to choose from:

Croissants
Yogurt
Bagels
Scones
Biscuits (in a can)
Pie (leftovers)
Muffins
Pizza (cold leftovers)
Corn bread
Cheese slices
Tomato slices
Avocado slices
Hash Brown Patties
Bananas
Cantaloupe
Honey Dew Melon
Watermelon
Grapes
Raisins
Strawberries
Berry berries
Toast

CHAPTER 2

APPETIZERS/SALADS/SIDES

An Appetizer sets the table of the stomach for further dining. Not to be confused with literally setting the table for dining, which we also highly recommend. Appetizers are the food that we eat to make us more hungry, just as Salads are the food we eat to tell ourselves we're being healthy. In reality an Appetizers is simply foreshadowing for an entrée. Literally a wetter of appetite. Appetizers doubtlessly have middle child syndrome: less responsibility than its older, larger, more heroically life-sustaining big brother Entrée, and WAY less adorable (see also: bacon-y) than everybody's little darling Brunch. Don't fret for appetizers though, thanks to their alliance with Sides and Salads, and an outstanding publicist, they have managed to become a critical component of Happy Hours everywhere.

IF YOU WANT TO DESTROY BRUSCHETTA

BRUSCHETTA WATCH OUT, CUZ I'M A WARM MUNCHIE

NOT EVERYONE KNOWS THIS,
BUT LIFE DOESN'T GET ANY BRUSCHETTA THAN THIS

1 24" baguette

3 Roma or heirloom tomatoes

1 tbsp fresh basil

1 tbsp olive oil

½ tsp oregano

1 tsp lemon juice

8 oz ball mozzarella

½ tbsp garlic

salt and pepper

sharp serrated knife

- Preheat oven to 350°F
- Slice bread into ¼" thick rounds with serrated knife and place on a baking sheet
- Coat each piece with a little olive oil
- Flip slices over, oil side down
- Toast in the oven for 5 minutes

- Rinse tomato, chop into ¼" cubes
- Mince garlic into smallest reasonable pieces
- Rinse basil, remove and discard stems, chop
- Combine tomatoes, basil, olive oil, oregano, garlic, and lemon juice in a 9" bowl and stir

- Slice mozzarella into ⅛" slices
- Cover each piece of bread with mozzarella
- With a fork, pick up some tomato mixture and put on each slice, leaving juice in bowl
- Top bread and cheese base with tomato mixture
- Sprinkle each bruschetta with salt and pepper
- Toast compiled bruschetta for 10 additional minutes
- All that's left is for *someone* to kiss the cook

ADVICE FROM A REAL LIVE GIRL:
CHICKS DIG FRESH BASIL. BE SURE TO KEEP YOUR
WINE GLASSES FULL WHILE YOU'RE COOKING THIS
DELICIOUS LITTLE FANCY TREAT.

NAPPATIZERS

ROLLSING WITH THE HOMIES

NOT EVERYONE KNOWS THIS, BUT THE "ROLL" IS THE SECOND MOST DELICIOUS FOOD SHAPE TO ONLY "ON A STICK"

1 package large flour tortillas
1 package sliced turkey
1 red beefsteak tomato
1 ripe avocado
1 package fresh basil
1 jar pitted green olives
1 box toothpicks
mayonnaise
hot chili sauce

- Spread mayo and/or hot chili sauce on tortilla
- Place a layer of turkey across tortilla
- Rinse tomato, slice ¼", line down tortilla's center
- Rinse avocado, remove stem and peel, slice thinly
- Apply sliced avocado parallel to the slices of meat
- Rinse basil, remove stems, line up across tortilla
- Roll tortilla and contents tightly
- Skewer resulting roll with toothpicks every 2 inches
- Place a single green olive on each toothpick
- Cut roughly equidistant between each toothpick
- All that's left is for *someone* to kiss the cook

ADVICE FROM A REAL LIVE GIRL:
DON'T PUT THE SAUCE TOO CLOSE TO THE EDGE OF
THE WRAP OR IT'LL SQUISH OUT.

GOT YOUR GOAT CHEESE TOASTIES

YOU'RE TOO GOUDA TO ME

NOT EVERYONE KNOWS THIS, BUT ANGLE CUTTING BREAD CAN ADD UP TO 20% MORE TOAST-ABLE SURFACE AREA, AND 50% MORE DELICIOUSNESS

1 24" baguette
2 tbsp olive oil
4 oz package of goat cheese
sharp serrated knife

•Preheat oven to 350°F
•Slice baguette into ¼" thick slices with knife
•Place on baking sheet close together
•Drizzle 1 tbsp olive oil over the bread slices
•Flip the pieces over and drizzle with remaining oil
•Put in the oven for 5-10 minutes or until toasty
•Meanwhile, put the goat cheese in a little bowl
•Put warm bread on a plate near the goat cheese
•Allow guest to spread the cheese on her bread
•All that's left is for *someone* to kiss the cook

ADVICE FROM A REAL LIVE GIRL:
THIS MIGHT SOUND FANCY, BUT IT'S VERY EASY
TO MAKE. THEN YOU GET CREDIT FOR MAKING
SOMETHING FANCY.

QUIN•OLÉ!

A QUICK QUINWALK ACROSS THE BORDER

NOT EVERYONE KNOWS THIS, BUT THE BEST WAY TO LET A GIRL KNOW SHE PHILS YOU WITH JOY IS TO PREPARE HER A SU-SU-PSEUDOCEREAL

1 cup quinoa

2 cups water

½ tsp salt

½ red bell pepper

½ green bell pepper

¼ cup white onion

8 oz canned black beans

1 tsp garlic

½ tsp chili powder

¼ tsp cumin

¼ tsp paprika

½ cup cilantro

1 tbsp olive oil

avocado (optional garnish)

- Combine quinoa, salt, and water in a pot
- Cover and bring to a boil on medium high
- Simmer covered on medium-low for 20 minutes then turn off
- Rinse peppers, remove stem/seeds, chop into ¼" cubes
- Rinse onion, remove top layer, chop a quarter of it into ¼" pieces
- Mince garlic into smallest reasonable pieces
- Rinse cilantro, discard stems, mince leaves
- Put all veggies, garlic, oil, and all spices in a 12" bowl
- After the quinoa is done cooking remove from heat
- Let the quinoa cool completely
- Add quinoa to 12" bowl with the beans and veggies
- Stir to combine all ingredients
- Slice avocado for garnish if using
- All that's left is for *someone* to kiss the cook

ADVICE FROM A REAL LIVE GIRL:
THE CHIPOTLE CHILLIES IN ADOBO SAUCE CAN BE FOUND IN A TINY CAN IN THE MEXICAN FOOD AISLE. THEY ARE NO JOKE! USE SPARINGLY.

QUINOAWESOME SALAD

A SALAD SO FRESH SHE'LL SWEAR IT HAS THREE HANDS

NOT EVERYONE KNOWS THIS, BUT THIS DISH IS LIKE THE GIN AND TONIC OF THE SALAD WORLD; LIGHT, REFRESHING, AND ALWAYS A GOOD IDEA

1 cup quinoa
2 cups water
¼ tsp salt
½ cup green peas
1 red beefsteak tomato
½ cucumber
½ cup cilantro
½ tsp dried thyme
½ tsp dried marjoram
1 lemon's juice
1 tbsp soy sauce

- Combine quinoa, salt, thyme, marjoram, and water in a pot
- Cover and bring to a boil on medium high
- Simmer covered on medium-low for 20 minutes then turn
  off
- Allow to cool
- Rinse and peel cucumber, dice into ¼" cubes
- Rinse tomato, dice into ¼" cubes
- Rinse cilantro, remove stems, and mince leaves
- Put all veggies and lemon juice in a 12" bowl
- Add cooled quinoa to the bowl with the veggies
- Stir thoroughly
- All that's left is for *someone* to kiss the cook

ADVICE FROM A REAL LIVE GIRL:
QUINOA CAN BE MADE IN A RICE COOKER, JUST LIKE
RICE. ADD QUINOA, WATER, AND PUSH THE BUTTON.

MIXED SIGNALS SALAD

LIKE A CLASSY NIGHT OUT ON THE TOWN, MORE FUN ALL DRESSED UP

NOT EVERYONE KNOWS THIS, BUT SPINACH IS TO MIXED SIGNAL SALAD AS PEANUTS ARE TO MIXED NUTS

1 bag spring mix greens (salad)

½ red bell pepper

2 tbsp red onion

4 tbsp candied pecans

4 tbsp goat cheese crumbles

½ pear

½ avocado

¼ cup dried cranberries

salad dressing, any vinaigrette

•Fill two salad bowls with spring mix
•Rinse red pepper, remove stem/seeds, chop into
 ¼" cubes
•Rinse onion, remove top layer, chop into ¼"
 cubes
•Rinse pear, remove stem/seeds, chop into ¼"
 cubes
•Rinse avocado, remove seed and peel, chop into
 ¼" cubes
•Put half the toppings on each salad
•Serve, with dressing on the side
•All that's left is for *someone* to kiss the cook

ADVICE FROM A REAL LIVE GIRL:
SERVING THE DRESSING ON THE SIDE IS IMPORTANT
HERE, AS PEOPLE HAVE VERY DIFFERENT IDEAS OF
WHAT A PROPERLY DRESSED SALAD IS.

ASIAN CARROT-E CHOP SALAD

I CARROT 'BOUT YOUR FEELINGS

NOT EVERYONE KNOWS THIS, BUT ASIA IS A REAL PLACE, AND WAS NOT NAMED AFTER AN 80'S BAND

2 carrots

1 head broccoli

3 tbsp cilantro

½ purple onion

1 red pepper

½ cup peanuts

1 fuji apple

3 tbsp peanut sauce

1 tsp hot sauce (optional)

- Rinse carrots, grate with cheese grater
- Rinse broccoli, chop crowns into ½" morsels
- Rinse cilantro, remove stems, and mince leaves
- Rinse onion, chop into ¼" cubes
- Rinse red pepper, remove stem/seeds, slice into ¼" strips
- Rinse apple, chop into ¼" cubes
- Combine all ingredients in a big serving bowl
- Stir contents until evenly coated with sauce
- All that's left is for *someone* to kiss the cook

ADVICE FROM A REAL LIVE GIRL:
PEANUT SAUCE CAN BE FOUND IN A LITTLE JAR IN
THE ASIAN FOOD AISLE.

MY BIG FAT GREEK SALAD

WHAT'S KALAMATA' WITH YOU?

NOT EVERYONE KNOWS THIS, BUT THE BEAV WAS RETICENT ABOUT ALLOWING ME TO CONTRIBUTE FOR FEAR IT WOULD "PRODUCE" SOME BAD PUNS.
FORTUNATELY IT DIDN'T.

1 pint cherry or grape tomatoes
1 cucumber
1 cup pitted kalamata olives
1 tbsp lemon juice
1 tbsp olive oil
2 tbsp chopped parsley
½ cup feta cheese
salt & pepper

•Rinse tomatoes and cut each one in half
•Rinse, peel, and dice cucumber into ¼" cubes
•Cut kalamata olive each in half
•Rinse parsley, remove stems, and chop leaves
tiny
•Combine all ingredients in a bowl and stir
•All that's left is for *someone* to kiss the cook

ADVICE FROM A REAL LIVE GIRL:
BUY TWICE AS MANY OLIVES AS YOU'LL NEED SO
YOU BOTH CAN SNACK ON THEM WHILE COOKING.

3 C'SER SALAD

DON'T DOUBT YOURSELF, YOU CAYENNE DO IT!

NOT EVERYONE KNOWS THIS, BUT THERE EXISTS A SMALL BUT DETERMINED GRASS ROOTS MOVEMENT TO MAKE CAYENNE THE OFFICIAL PEPPER OF CHEYENNE, WY. IT'S A 'HOTLY' CONTESTED DEBATE.

½ purple cabbage head

2 large carrots

1 tsp dijon mustard

¼ cup apple cider vinegar

1 tsp honey

1 tsp salt

¼ tsp cayenne pepper

3 tbsp olive oil

- Rinse cabbage, cut in half, remove tough center
- Slice remaining cabbage into ⅛" noodle-like bits
- Rinse carrots, grate with cheese grater
- Put cabbage & carrots in a large serving bowl
- Combine and mix all other ingredients in a 6" bowl
- Pour over cabbage and carrots, toss to coat
- All that's left is for *someone* to kiss the cook

ADVICE FROM A REAL LIVE GIRL:
MAY I RECOMMEND THIS WITH THE SLOPPY JOES
ON PAGE 152?

CARMEN MIRANDA RIGHTS FRUIT SALAD

SHE PROBABLY WASN'T GOING TO GET SCURVY ANYWAY, BUT NOW SHE HAS
YOU TO THANK FOR IT.

> NOT EVERYONE KNOWS THIS, BUT FRUIT WAS FIRST WORN AS A HAT
> IN BATTLE AS ARMOR BY THE LIOT PEOPLE. NEVER HEARD OF THEM?
> NOT SURPRISINGLY THEY'RE EXTINCT NOW (I MEAN, FRUIT AS ARMOR
> PEOPLE?!)

1 grapefruit

1 orange

1 apple

1 pear

2 kiwis

2 tbsp fresh basil

1 cup cashews

- Rinse each fruit and remove the peels (optional to peel apple and pear)
- Remove the seeds and cores from all but the kiwis
- Chop all fruit into ½" cubes
- Wash basil, remove stems, and chop tiny
- Chop or crush cashews into ¼" pieces
- Combine all above items in a large serving bowl
- Stir to cover all bits well with citrus juices
- All that's left is for *someone* to kiss the cook

ADVICE FROM A REAL LIVE GIRL:
KIWI STEMS ARE A BIT ROUGH. BE SURE TO CHOP
THEM OUT. THE CITRUS JUICE WILL PRESERVE THE
APPLE AND PEAR.

ARUGULAMAZING SALAD

IT WOULD BE ARUDE...GULA NOT TO ACCEPT

NOT EVERYONE KNOWS THIS, BUT ARUGULA USED TO BE IN A SERIOUS RELATIONSHIP WITH KALE, BUT THEY BROKE UP AND ARUGULA HAS BEEN 'A LITTLE BITTER' EVER SINCE

4 cups arugula
2 cups strawberries
1 tbsp balsamic vinegar
1 tbsp olive oil
½ cup goat cheese crumbles
salt & pepper

•Rinse arugula and strawberries
•Remove strawberry stems, chop into ½" morsels
•Combine oil, vinegar, salt and pepper in a small
  bowl
•Place arugula in a 12" bowl and add
  strawberries
•Pour dressing over salad in bowl
•Toss salad gently until strawberries are
  dispersed and dressing coats
•Divide between two salad bowls
•Top with goat cheese and serve
•All that's left is for *someone* to kiss the cook

ADVICE FROM A REAL LIVE GIRL:
THE ORIGINAL TITLE FOR THIS SALAD WAS
"RESTAURANT SALAD."
IT'S JUST THAT GOOD.

MARINARA SALAD

DELICIOUSNESS LIKE THIS DOESN'T HAPPEN BY SNACCIDENT

NOT EVERYONE KNOWS THIS, BUT SOME MEATS BECOME MORE DELICIOUS WHEN SOAKED IN SAUCE. I'M GONNA LET YOU 'MARINARANADE' ON THAT THOUGHT FOR A BIT.

1 pint cherry or grape tomatoes

2 sprigs fresh basil

1 8 oz ball mozzarella (about a tennis ball size)

3 tbsp olive oil

¼ tsp salt

¼ tsp pepper

- Wash tomatoes and cut each one in half
- Remove basil leaves from stems and chop tiny
- Chop mozzarella into ¼ " bite-size cubes
- Put all ingredients in a 9" bowl
- Stir to coat
- Serve
- All that's left is for *someone* to kiss the cook

ADVICE FROM A REAL LIVE GIRL:
THIS SIDE DISH IS GREAT WITH STEAK, PAGE 146.
BUT LET'S FACE IT, WHAT ISN'T?

HOW DO YOU LIKE THEM APPLES
SPINACH SALAD
THIS SALAD IS NOT TO BE DIPPED IN CARAMEL, I ASKED

NOT EVERYONE KNOWS THIS, BUT THERE ARE A FINITE NUMBER OF FUNNY JOKES ABOUT SALAD AND THIS COOKBOOK EXCEEDED THAT NUMBER SEVERAL JOKES AGO

4 cups fresh spinach
1 apple
½ cup cashews
¼ cup raisins
1 tbsp brown sugar
1 tbsp olive oil
1 tbsp balsamic vinegar

•Rinse spinach and remove stems
•Rinse apples, peel, remove stem and core
•Chop apples into ¼" cubes
•Put spinach, apples, cashews, and raisins into a 12" serving bowl
•In a 6" bowl mix brown sugar, olive oil, and vinegar
•Pour olive oil mixture over salad and toss
•Divide between two salad bowls
•All that's left is for *someone* to kiss the cook

ADVICE FROM A REAL LIVE GIRL:
PULL ANY BIG STEMS OFF THE SPINACH AND
THROW THEM OUT.

SIMPLE GREEN SALAD

TAKE THIS SALAD AS A SIMPLE OF OUR LOVE

NOT EVERYONE KNOWS THIS, BUT A GREEN SALAD IS WHAT HAPPENS WHEN A VARIETY OF GARNISHES SNUGGLE

4 cups salad greens
1 cup cherry tomatoes
1 cup croutons
½ cup grated parmesan cheese
balsamic vinegar salad dressing

•Rinse the salad greens
•Rinse tomatoes and cut each in half
•Divide the salad greens between two salad
  bowls
•Top with the tomatoes, croutons, and cheese
•Serve with dressing on the side
•All that's left is for *someone* to kiss the cook

ADVICE FROM A REAL LIVE GIRL:
IF USING SPINACH AND YOU SEE ANY BIG STEMS,
TEAR THEM OFF AND THROW THEM OUT.

INGREDIENTS SALAD

CHICKS DIG INGREDIENTS

NOT EVERYONE KNOWS THIS,
BUT INGREDIENTS ARE THE SPICE OF LIFE

15 oz canned corn

6 oz fresh raspberries

½ cup red onion

15 oz canned black beans

1 ripe avocado

1 red beefsteak tomato

½ bunch cilantro

1 tbsp olive oil

1 lime's juice

salt and pepper to taste

For serving: 1 bag hearty corn chips

•Drain liquid out of the corn and beans

•Put corn and beans in a 12" serving bowl

•Rinse raspberries and add to the bowl

•Rinse, remove seed and peel of avocado

•Dice avocado into ¼" cubes

•Rinse tomato, remove stem, and dice into ¼" cubes

•Rinse cilantro, remove stems, and chop tiny

•Rinse onion, remove outler layer, and chop into ¼" cubes

•Combine all ingredients into a 12" bowl

•Toss well to coat

•Season with salt and pepper to taste

•Serve with hearty corn chips

•All that's left is for *someone* to kiss the cook

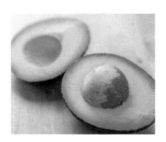

ADVICE FROM A REAL LIVE GIRL:
THIS RECIPE DEMONSTRATES THAT YOU HAVE A
SOPHISTICATED PALETTE. IF YOU DON'T ACTUALLY
HAVE ONE,
JUST PRETEND.

CHICKS DIG IT SALAD

I'D RATHER BE IN THE GARBONZONE THAN THE FRIEND ZONE

NOT EVERYONE KNOWS THIS, BUT JUST BEFORE HARVEST THE GARBANZO BEAN IS NATURE'S MARACA.

2 tbsp fresh mint
15 oz can chickpeas
1 tbsp olive oil
¼ cup golden raisins
¼ cup red wine vinegar
salt & pepper

•Rinse mint, remove stems, and mince leaves
•Drain chickpeas
•Put all ingredients in a 12" bowl
•Stir thoroughly to coat evenly
•Salt and pepper to taste
•All that's left is for *someone* to kiss the cook

ADVICE FROM A REAL LIVE GIRL:
FRESH MINT MAKES YOU SEEM FANCY AND SOPHISTICATED.

SO EASY A MAN CAN DO IT BEAN SALAD

BEAN THERE, DONE THAT

NOT EVERYONE KNOWS THIS, BUT THE MAN-MADE BEAN SALAD ORIGINATED IN MESOAMERICA AS EARLY AS 8000 TO 5000 B.C., MOMENTS LATER, SO DID THE "5 SECOND RULE."

15 oz canned kidney beans
15 oz canned black beans
15 oz canned garbanzo beans
¼ red onion
1 tsp curry powder
½ cup fresh parsley
1 tbsp garlic
1 lemon's juice
¼ cup olive oil
salt and pepper

- Rinse and drain all beans and put in 12" serving bowl
- Rinse onion, remove top layer, chop a quarter of it into ¼" pieces
- Combine all remaining ingredients in serving bowl
- Stir to coat all ingredients in oil/juice
- Salt and pepper to taste
- All that's left is for *someone* to kiss the cook

ADVICE FROM A REAL LIVE GIRL:
IF YOU DON'T HAVE A STRAINER, USE THE LID OF
THE CAN TO DRAIN THE JUICE. THEN FILL WITH
WATER, SWISH,
AND DRAIN AGAIN.

I HOPE YOU PACKED A-SPARE-AGUS

WHAT AN ACCIDENTLY ELECTROCUTED VEGETABLE WOULD LOOK LIKE

NOT EVERYONE KNOWS THIS, BUT IF VEGETABLES EVER PARTICIPATED IN MEDIEVAL JOUSTING TOURNAMENTS, ASPARAGUS WOULD FUNCTION AS THE LANCES

1 lb/bunch asparagus
1 tbsp olive oil
½ lemon
salt & pepper

•Preheat the oven to 425°F
•Rinse asparagus, cut/discard bottom 2" of stem
•Line oven safe baking sheet with foil
•Place asparagus on sheet in a single layer
•Drizzle with olive oil
•Cut lemon in half and squeeze half over it
•Sprinkle with salt & pepper
•Bake in oven for 15 minutes
•All that's left is for *someone* to kiss the cook

ADVICE FROM A REAL LIVE GIRL:
IF YOU OVER COOK THE ASPARAGUS,
IT'LL GET STRINGY.
BE CAREFUL.

AN HONORABLE CUMINTION

YOU TWO WERE CUMIN'T FOR EACH OTHER

*NOT EVERYONE KNOWS THIS, BUT CUMIN CREDITS PARSLEY AS A
LIFE-COACH DURING ITS FORMATIVE YEARS,
A CUMINTOR IF YOU WILL*

1 lb baby carrots
3 tbsp olive oil
2 tsp cumin
salt & pepper

- Preheat oven to 425°F
- Rinse carrots and put in 12" bowl
- Drizzle with olive oil
- Sprinkle with the cumin, salt, and pepper
- Stir
- Spread on baking sheet in a single layer
- Bake 25 minutes until carrots are tender
- All that's left is for *someone* to kiss the cook

ADVICE FROM A REAL LIVE GIRL:
USE TIN FOIL ON THE BAKING SHEET FOR EASIER
CLEAN UP.

SWEET FRITES

DON'T BE AFRAID TO SHOW HER YOUR SWEET SIDE-DISH

> NOT EVERYONE KNOWS THIS, BUT BEFORE THE 1860'S THE SOUTH'S UNOFFICIAL MANTRA WAS "IF AT FIRST YOU DON'T SECEDE, FRY AND FRY AGAIN

2 sweet potatoes

2 tbsp olive oil

1 tsp salt

1 tsp pepper

2 tsp rosemary

1 tsp curry powder

1 garlic clove

¼ red onion

- Preheat oven to 350°F
- Rinse potatoes and peel
- Cut potatoes into fry-shaped and sized wedges
- Mince garlic into smallest reasonable pieces
- Rinse onion, remove top layer, chop into ¼" pieces
- Put all ingredients in a 12" bowl and stir
- Bake on foil lined baking sheet for 30 minutes or until tender
- Serve with ketchup if desired
- All that's left is for *someone* to kiss the cook

ADVICE FROM A REAL LIVE GIRL:
CALL AN AUDIBLE: SERVE WITH
DON'T CURRY, BE HAPPY, PAGE 130.

DON'T CURRY, BE HAPPY, PAGE 130.

MATERS, TATERS, & OLIVE...ATERS

OLIVE ME, WHY NOT TAKE OLIVE ME...

NOT EVERYONE KNOWS THIS, BUT THIS VEGETABLE SALAD CONTAINS TWO FRUITS AND A STARCH; THEREFORE ARGUABLY NO VEGETABLES WHATSOEVER

1 lb little multi color potatoes
1 pint cherry or grape tomatoes
4 cloves garlic
1 tsp rosemary
½ tsp salt
½ tsp pepper
2 tbsp olive oil
½ cup <u>pitted</u> kalamata olives

- Preheat oven to 375°
- Rinse potatoes and chop into ½" cubes
- Mince garlic into smallest reasonable pieces
- Chop rosemary into tiny pieces
- Combine potatoes, garlic, rosemary, salt, pepper, and oil in a 12" bowl
- Stir to combine
- Spray a large baking dish with cooking spray
- Spread coated potatoes in baking dish
- Bake for 20 minutes
- Rinse tomatoes
- Cut each tomato and olive in half
- Flip & stir potatoes
- Add tomatoes and olives on top
- Bake for an additional 25-30 minutes
- Potatoes should be easy to poke with fork
- Transfer to a serving bowl and allow to cool
- All that's left is for *someone* to kiss the cook

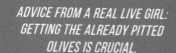

ADVICE FROM A REAL LIVE GIRL: GETTING THE ALREADY PITTED OLIVES IS CRUCIAL.

ONCE BAKED POTATOES

BECAUSE TWICE BAKED POTATOES ARE SOMETIMES ONE BAKE TOO MANY

NOT EVERYONE KNOWS THIS, BUT THE BEAV WAS SUPPOSED TO REMIND ME TO PUT IN MORE POTATO-BASED RECIPES, ALAS WE'VE BOTH LONG SINCE F'AU GRATIN

2 big potatoes
aluminum foil

Toppings Bar:
cheddar cheese
chopped chives
bacon bits
sour cream
butter
salt & pepper

- Pre-heat the oven to 350°F
- Rinse potatoes
- Stab each potato 10 times with a fork
- Wrap potatoes in foil
- Bake in the oven for 1 hour
- Meanwhile, set up the toppings bar
     - Grate cheese
     - Chop chives
     - Put each topping bar item into tiny bowls
- Remove (Use a pot holder; literally "hot potato")
- Unwrap, place one potato on each plate
- Cut a slice in the top and squish to open it up
- Top with desired toppings
- All that's left is for *someone* to kiss the cook

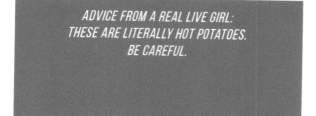
ADVICE FROM A REAL LIVE GIRL:
THESE ARE LITERALLY HOT POTATOES.
BE CAREFUL.

S'MASHED POTATOES

YOU WOULDN'T LIKE ME WHEN I'M HUNGRY

NOT EVERYONE KNOWS THIS, BUT THE ACT OF "MASHING" A POTATO WAS THE FIRST KNOWN INSTANCE OF GETTING AWAY WITH "PLAYING WITH YOUR FOOD"

2 big potatoes
2 cloves garlic
½ cup milk
3 tbsp butter
½ tsp salt
½ tsp pepper
½ cup cheddar cheese

- Rinse, peel, and chop the potatoes into ½"
  cubes
- Mince garlic into smallest reasonable pieces
- Bring a 12" pot of water to a boil
- Once boiling, add potatoes
- Boil for about 20 minutes until easily pierced
  with a fork
- Meanwhile, place all other ingredients in 12"
  bowl

- Drain potatoes and place bowl
- Mash until all ingredients are combined
- All that's left is for *someone* to kiss the cook

ADVICE FROM A REAL LIVE GIRL:
IT'S OK TO LEAVE A LITTLE BIT OF THE PEELS ON.
EXTRA FIBER.

SPUDDY BUDDIES

WHEN LIFE GIVES YOU POTATOES...BUT VODKA IS NOT AN OPTION...

> *NOT EVERYONE KNOWS THIS, BUT THE FIRST POTATO SALAD DATES*
> *BACK TO THE VERY FIRST BAR-B-QUE*

1 ½ lb red potatoes
¼ cup parsley leaves
¼ cup white onion
½ cup olive oil
2 tbsp white wine vinegar
1 heaping tsp fancy brown mustard
½ tsp paprika
salt & pepper

•Rinse and chop potatoes into ½" cubes
•Cover potatoes in a 8" pot with water
•Add a tsp of salt and bring to a boil on high
•Reduce heat (medium) to boil for 15 minutes
•Rinse parsley, remove stems, and mince leaves
•Rinse onion, remove top layer, chop into ¼"
 pieces
•Put all ingredients except potatoes into 12"
serving bowl
•Turn the heat off of the potatoes
•Drain the water out of the potatoes
•Put potatoes in the 12" bowl and stir to combine
•Put in fridge to chill for an hour if there's time
•All that's left is for *someone* to kiss the cook

ADVICE FROM A REAL LIVE GIRL:
A LIGHT DUSTING OF PAPRIKA OVER THE POTATO
SALAD ADDS A TOUCH OF CLASS.

BRING IT CROUTON

IT'S LIKE BREAD STICKS WITH THE CRUSTS CUT OFF

NOT EVERYONE KNOWS THIS, BUT CROUTONS CAN DOUBLE AS DOG TREATS - THE WAY TO A MAN'S HEART IS THROUGH HIS STOMACH, THE WAY TO A WOMAN'S HEART IS THROUGH HER DOG'S STOMACH

2 bread ends from sandwich bread
2 tbsp olive oil
salt & pepper

•Preheat oven to 350°
•Cut bread ends into crouton-sized pieces
•Put in a 12" bowl and pour olive oil over the top
•Sprinkle with salt & pepper
•Stir to coat
•Spread croutons on a baking sheet in a single layer
•Bake 15 minutes, until crunchy

ADVICE FROM A REAL LIVE GIRL:
HOME MADE CROUTONS ARE BALLER.

A POSITIVE SPINACH

DON'T SPIN(ACH) ALL IN ONE PLACE

NOT EVERYONE KNOWS THIS, BUT SPINACH WAS ONCE CONSIDERED IN ONE PLANT FAMILY, BUT IN 2003 IT WAS MERGED INTO SOME OTHER PLANT FAMILY, AND NOW THOSE FAMILY REUNIONS ARE SUPER(FOOD) AWKWARD

10 oz spinach
1 tbsp olive oil
1/3 cup heavy cream
1/8 tsp salt
1/8 tsp pepper

•Put olive oil and spinach in a 12" skillet
•Cook and stir on medium until spinach has wilted
•Add cream, salt, and pepper
•Cook for 3 more minutes
•All that's left is for *someone* to kiss the cook

ADVICE FROM A REAL LIVE GIRL:
10 OZ LOOKS LIKE AN ABSURD AMOUNT OF
SPINACH, BUT IT WILL COOK DOWN A LOT. IF THERE
ARE ANY BIG STEMS,
REMOVE THEM AND THROW AWAY.

BAKED TOMATOES

IT'S LIKE A WARM BLOODY MARY IN SOLID FORM

*NOT EVERYONE KNOWS THIS, BUT SHARKMATO WAS
RELEASED EXCLUSIVELY FOR INTERNET DOWNLOAD.
SO. MANY. MEGABITES...*

2 red beefsteak tomatoes
⅓ cup bread crumbs, any kind
1 tbsp garlic
3 tbsp parsley
1 tbsp olive oil

•Preheat the oven to 350°F
•Rinse tomatoes, cut in half
•Remove seeds with a spoon
•Place tomatoes cut side up in a baking dish
•Rinse parsley, remove stems, and mince leaves
•Mince garlic into smallest reasonable pieces
•Mix garlic, bread crumbs, and parsley in a 4"
 bowl
•Spread mixture over the top of tomatoes
•Drizzle with olive oil
•Remove from oven and allow to cool
•All that's left is for *someone* to kiss the cook

ADVICE FROM A REAL LIVE GIRL:
BREAD CRUMBS ARE A THING YOU BUY AT THE
STORE IN A LITTLE PAPER CANISTER. THEY ARE
NOT THE SAME AS THE BREAD YOU HAVE AT HOME.

GREEN WITH ENVY BEANS

IT IS EASY BEING GREEN

NOT EVERYONE KNOWS THIS, BUT GREEN BEANS ARE IRONICALLY STILL NOT YET CONVINCED ABOUT THIS WHOLE "GLOBAL WARMING" THING

32 oz canned plain green beans

2 tbsp garlic

1 tsp dried dill

¼ sweet yellow onion

1 bouillon cube, any flavor

1 tsp salt

1 tsp pepper

•Drain green beans
•Mince garlic into smallest reasonable pieces
•Rinse onion, remove top layer, chop into ¼"
  pieces
•Put all ingredients in a pot
•Fill pot with water until green beans are
  covered
•Bring to a boil
•Boil for 7 minutes until onions looks clear
•Use a slotted spoon or fork to serve green
beans
•All that's left is for *someone* to kiss the cook

ADVICE FROM A REAL LIVE GIRL:
THESE GREEN BEANS ARE WAY BETTER ON THE
DAY AFTER YOU COOK THEM. SO IF YOU HAVE THEM
LEFTOVER, ENJOY!
BOUILLON ISN'T SCARY. ASK YOUR
GRANDMA WHERE TO FIND IT AT THE
GROCERY STORE.

CREAM OF THE CROP CORN

DO SOME OF THESE TITLES SEEM A LITTLE CORNY TO YOU?

NOT EVERYONE KNOWS THIS, BUT DESPITE THE FACT THAT CORN COMES FROM "AMERICA'S HEARTLAND" IT IS TERRIBLE FOR AMERICAN'S HEARTS

30 oz canned whole kernel corn
½ cup heavy cream
salt & pepper

•Drain excess liquids from canned corn
•Put all ingredients in a 12" skillet
•Bring to a boil, then reduce to low
•Stir for 10 minutes
•All that's left is for *someone* to kiss the cook

SNACKHACKS

APPETIZERS, SIDES, & SALADS

Some food components, or "snacks" if you will, are so literally self-explanatory (the directions are simple and right on the box) that they don't warrant a recipe; however, it's a useful resource to have a list of options/ideas to choose from:

Mixed Greens
Carrot Sticks
Celery Sticks
Apple Slices
Orange slices
Cheese slices
Crackers
Cured sausage
Olive bar
Mixed nuts
Cashews
Almonds
Wild Rice (box)
Jambalaya (box)
Spanish Rice (box)
Red Beans and Rice (box)
Mexican Style Rice (box)
Herb & Butter Rice (box)
Fried Rice (box)
Fancy chips
7 Layer Dip
Corn bread (box)

CHAPTER 3

DRESSINGS & DIPS

Dressings and Dips perform the same function; to make things that on their own would taste like penance taste like awesomeness instead. Whether poured on, soaked in, or dipped into, Dressing and Dips are commonly solely responsible for adding flavor, texture, and the only hint of deliciousness to salad, vegetables, chips, and crackers alike! Together they are like the bacon-wrapped of the vegetable world; a dynamic duo shielding humanity from the drab, tasteless, compromising mediocrity of otherwise healthy plants and grains alike.

LITTLE BLACK DRESSING

IT'S SLIMMING, SIMPLE, ELEGANT, TIMELESS, AND CAN BE DRESSED UP OR DRESSED DOWN DEPENDING ON THE OCCASION

NOT EVERYONE KNOWS THIS BUT, LITTLE BLACK DRESSING IS THE CHUCKMAN'S FAVORITE...
BUT PROBABLY ONLY BECAUSE "SUMMER DRESSING" HAS YET TO BE INVENTED

¼ cup balsamic vinegar

½ cup olive oil

1 tbsp garlic

1 tsp brown sugar

½ tsp salt

½ tsp pepper

•Chop garlic as finely as is reasonable to yeild 1 tbsp

•Mix the ingredients together in a small bowl

•Stir vigorously before serving over salad

•All that's left is for *someone* to kiss the cook

THE BEE'S KNEES
HONEY MUSTARD VINAIGRETTE
MR. MUSTARD, IN THE CONSERVATORY, WITH THE CANDLESTICK

*NOT EVERYONE KNOWS THIS, BUT VINAIGRETTES ARE THREE PARTS OIL,
ONE PART VINEGAR,
AND 37 PARTS SWEET, SWEET LOVE*

4 tbsp dijon mustard
¼ cup honey
¼ cup cider vinegar
1 ½ tsp salt
⅓ cup olive oil

•Get out a 6" bowl
•Put all ingredients in bowl and stir
•Serve with salad
•All that's left is for *someone* to kiss the cook

ADVICE FROM A REAL LIVE GIRL:
YOU CAN SUBSTITUTE THIS DRESSING FOR THE
HOMEMADE ONE IN THE APPLE SPINACH SALAD
RECIPE, PAGE 82. IT MAKES A LOT, STORE
LEFTOVERS IN A JAR IN THE FRIDGE.

THE CHUCKMAN'S ALL-PURPOSE MARINADE

FOR USE EXCLUSIVELY ON ELK STEAKS. J/K.

NOT EVERYONE KNOWS THIS, BUT MY JOKES ARE A LOT LIKE MARINADE, BEST IF YOU LET THEM SOAK IN FOR LONGER THAN YOU'D RATHER HAVE TO WAIT

1 gallon zipping freezer bag

1 cup red wine

¼ cup soy sauce

¼ cup Worcestershire sauce

2 tbsp dijon mustard

2 tbsp honey

1 tsp minced garlic

1 tsp black pepper

¼ cup olive oil

2 sprigs fresh rosemary

juice of 1 lemon

- Mince garlic into smallest reasonable pieces
- Combine above ingredients in bag
- Place steaks in bag, zip it until it locks
- Shake it all up together (gently so as not to leak)
- Place in refrigerator for 24 hours (or so)
- Make sure meat is submerged
- Reposition periodically if not submerged
- Open carefully
- Use leftover marinade tomorrow on chicken (optional)
- All that's left is for *someone* to kiss the cook

ADVICE FROM A REAL LIVE GIRL:
YOU CAN USE THIS MARINADE IN PLACE OF THE SAUCE FOR
NOT A MISS STEAK, PAGE 146

A BRIE...F HISTORY OF JAM

THIS IS WHAT A WARM SUMMER BRIEZE TASTES LIKE

NOT EVERYONE KNOWS THIS, BUT SERVING SAID DISH WITH A LESSER CHEESE WOULD BE A BRIECH IN PROTOCOL

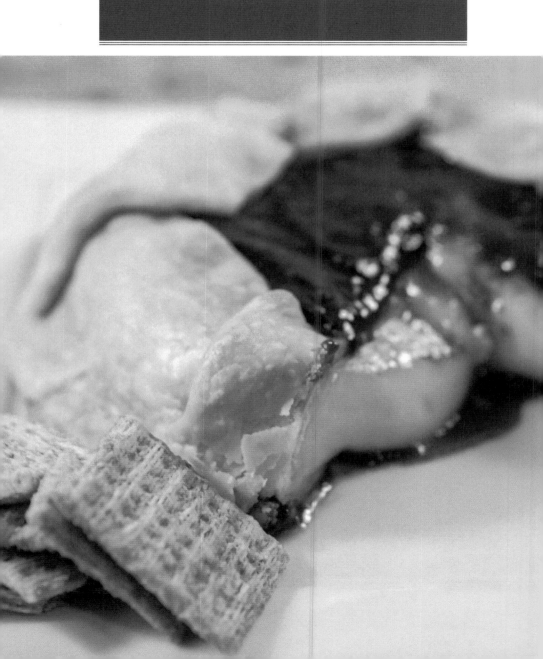

8 oz wheel of brie cheese

1 ready made pie crust

1 ½ cups raspberry jam

1 toothpick (optional)

1 box of fancy hearty dipping crackers

•Preheat oven to 400°F
•Spray a baking sheet with nonstick cooking oil
•Lay out one pie crust on baking sheet
•Pour ¾ cup jam on center of pie crust
•Place unwrapped wheel of brie cheese on jam
•Pour remaining ¾ cup jam on center of brie wheel
•Fold edges of crust together towards the center

•Push crust edges firmly down in center of brie
•Pin edges at center with toothpick
•Bake for 18 minutes (until crust is golden brown)
•Allow to cool for at least 5 minutes
•All that's left is for *someone* to kiss the cook

ADVICE FROM A REAL LIVE GIRL:
THE MERE FACT YOU KNOW WHAT BRIE IS, IS LIKELY
ENOUGH TO IMPRESS WOMEN.

UNCLE SAUL'S SOLVES ALL SALSA

IT'S THE NEW HOTNESS

NOT EVERYONE KNOWS THIS, BUT THIS SALSA LITERALLY SOLVES ALL YOUR PROBLEMS...SO LONG AS ALL OF YOUR PROBLEMS ARE BLAND TORTILLA CHIP RELATED

3 tomatoes

1 onion

1 garlic clove

15 oz canned black beans

15 oz canned corn

1 jalapeno

3 tbsp lime juice

1 tsp salt

1 tsp pepper

½ cup cilantro

•Rinse tomatoes, dice into ⅛" cubes
•Rinse onion, remove top layer, chop into ⅛"
 pieces
•Mince garlic into smallest bits reasonable
•Drain and rinse canned black beans
•Drain and rinse canned corn
•Rinse jalapeno, remove stem and seeds, mince
•Rinse cilantro, remove stems, and mince leaves
•Combine above ingredients in a bowl
•Stir thoroughly to mix and moisten uniformly
•All that's left is for *someone* to kiss the cook

ADVICE FROM A REAL LIVE GIRL:
IF YOU CAN MAKE THIS THE DAY BEFORE YOUR
DATE, IT CAN "JUICE" OVERNIGHT AND IS MUCH
TASTIER.

DON'T CURRY, BE HAPPY

THIS PUN JUST ACURRIED TO ME

NOT EVERYONE KNOWS THIS, BUT THOSE LITTLE BOWL-LIKE CONTAINERS RESTAURANTS PROVIDE DIPPING SAUCES IN ARE CALLED RAMEKINS.

½ cup regular ketchup
1 tbsp curry powder

•Put the curry powder in a small bowl
•Add ketchup and stir to combine
•Serve with anything you'd like to see dipped in
 ketchup
•All that's left is for *someone* to kiss the cook

ADVICE FROM A REAL LIVE GIRL:
THIS WILL MAKE YOU LOOK LIKE A
GENIUS. OR A RESTAURATEUR.
YET, IT'S SO SIMPLE.

WAITING FOR MANGOT

THE LADY-PEACH STARTED TALKING ABOUT COMMITMENT,
YOU SHOULD HAVE SEEN THAT MAN-GO.

NOT EVERYONE KNOWS THIS, BUT THE WORD SALSA MEANS SAUCE...AND MANGO SAUCE SOUNDS LIKE A REALLY, REALLY GOOD IDEA

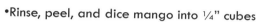

1 ripe mango
1 tomato
½ red onion
1 jalapeno
1 tbsp lime juice
¼ cup cilantro, chopped small

•Rinse, peel, and dice mango into ¼" cubes
•Rinse tomato, chop into ¼" cubes
•Rinse onion, remove top layer, chop into ⅛" pieces
•Rinse jalapeno, remove stem and seeds, mince
•Combine all ingredients in a bowl and stir
•All that's left is for *someone* to kiss the cook

ADVICE FROM A REAL LIVE GIRL:
BE SURE TO GET A SOFT, RIPE MANGO.
IF YOU GET AN UNRIPE ONE, NO AMOUNT OF BRUTE
FORCE CAN TURN IT INTO SALSA.

GUACAHOLYMOLE

ITS 6.022×10^{23} OF DELICIOUSNESS

NOT EVERYONE KNOWS THIS, BUT GUACAMOLE IS LITERALLY THE MOST DELICIOUS THING ONE CAN DIP SOMETHING ELSE IN... UNTIL BACON DIP IS A THING

3 avocados

1 ripe red beefsteak tomato

½ white onion

¼ cup cilantro

2 tsp lemon juice

¼ tsp salt

¼ tsp pepper

- Remove seed and peel of avocados
- In a small bowl whip avocado meat into paste
- Rinse tomato, chop into ⅛" cubes
- Rinse onion, remove top layer, chop into ⅛" cubes
- Rinse cilantro, remove stems, and mince leaves
- Combine all ingredients in a bowl and stir
- All that's left is for *someone* to kiss the cook

ADVICE FROM A REAL LIVE GIRL:
IF YOU LEAVE ONE OF THE AVOCADO SEEDS IN THE
BOWL, YOUR LEFTOVER GUACAMOLE WON'T TURN
BROWN IN THE FRIDGE OVERNIGHT.

TOP NOTCH TAPENADE

OLIVE FOR THIS STUFF

NOT EVERYONE KNOWS THIS, BUT IF YOU SPREAD THIS ON TURKEY YOU WILL PROBABLY EVENTUALLY TAPENOD-OFF

1 container of olive tapenade (from store)
fresh parsley
bread or cracker vessel for serving

•Pour it into one of your small serving bowls
•Rinse parsley, remove stems, and mince leaves
•Place fresh parsley on top
•All that's left is for *someone* to kiss the cook

ADVICE FROM A REAL LIVE GIRL:
OLIVE TAPENADE IS DELICIOUS,
BUT A BEAR TO MAKE. SO WE THINK YOU SHOULD
JUST BUY SOME AND PRETEND YOU MADE IT. SERVE
WITH TOASTED BAGUETTE SLICES, PITA BREAD, OR
WITH CRACKERS.

MR. RON'S (TECHNICALLY NOT) CHEESE DIP

DELICIOUS X SATISFYING = PASTEURIZED PROCESSED CHEESE 'PRODUCT'

*NOT EVERYONE KNOWS THIS, BUT BEFORE DIP WAS
INVENTED CHIPS WERE USED AS A FORM OF TORTURE...
NOT THE WORLD'S WORST FORM, BUT STILL, UNPLEASANT*

1 brick pasteurized processed cheese product
30 oz canned diced tomatoes and chilies
strong, hearty chips for serving

•Cut "cheese" into 1" cubes
•Place into a large microwave safe bowl
•Drain 1 (of 2) can diced tomatoes and chilies
•Pour both cans over the cheese
•Microwave for 5 minutes, stir
•Microwave another 5 minutes, stir
•Serve with strong/hearty chips
•All that's left is for *someone* to kiss the cook

ADVICE FROM A REAL LIVE GIRL:
OPTIONAL: COOK UP A 1/2 POUND OF BREAKFAST
SAUSAGE AND ADD FOR EXTRA DECADENCE. COVER
WHEN MICROWAVING OR IT'LL SPATTER.

SNACKHACKS

Some food components, or "snacks" if you will, are so literally self-explanatory (the directions are simple and right on the box) that they don't warrant a recipe; however, it's a useful resource to have a list of options/ideas to choose from:

Salad dressings:
Balsamic vinegar
Blue cheese dressing
Caesar salad
Creamy Italian dressing
French dressing
Ginger dressing
Italian dressing
Oil and vinegar
Ranch dressing
Raspberry vinaigrette
Russian dressing
Salad cream
Salad oils
Thousand Island dressing
Traditional Balsamic Vinegar
Vinaigrette

Dips:

Aioli
Artichoke dip
Baba ghanoush
Barbecue sauce
Bean dip
Buffalo sauce
Chile con queso
Chocolate
Chutney
Clam dip
Cocktail sauce

French onion dip
Fruit dip
Fry sauce
Garlic butter sauce
Gravy
Guacamole
Hazelnut butter
Honey
Hot sauce
Hummus
Jus

Ketchup
Marinara sauce
Mayonnaise
Mustard
Nacho cheese dip
Salsa
Soy Sauce
Spinach dip
Tartar Sauce

CHAPTER 4

ENTRÉES

Abandon hope all ye who entrée here. Just kidding, hope spring (rolls) eternal, it's kind of the whole point of this book. I can show you the world, take you hunger by hunger... but I digest. The entrée is the centerpiece of a meal, metaphorically speaking the meat of the matter if you will. (Note: It's also often literally the meat, whether you will or not.) Entrées are the big show, center stage, the main event, and any other flattering metaphor one may chose to denote grandeur and centricity. In short, don't screw this up. In long, here is your chance to dazzle, wow, and impress your lady friend with life sustaining sustenance. It doesn't get much more super-heroic than that; I bet she didn't even know she was dining with a super hero! You go boy.

Aside: Some of our readers have raised concerns about a troubling lack of an excess of food related puns in this chapter. Your concerns have been andouille noted.

THE PRINCESS AND THE CHICKPEA STEW

ONE PLUS ONE MAKES STEW

NOT EVERYONE KNOWS THIS, BUT STEW WAS INVENTED BY SOMEONE WHO REALIZED THEY'D BE HUNGRY LATER

30 oz canned chickpeas

8 oz canned corn

8 oz canned peas

1 orange bell pepper

1 ripe red beefsteak tomato

2 cloves garlic

1 tbsp curry powder

½ white onion

½ tbsp chili powder

1 tbsp butter

¼ tsp cumin

2 cups chicken broth

•Drain water out of canned chickpeas
•Drain water out of canned corn
•Drain water out of canned peas
•Rinse pepper, remove stem & seeds, chop into ¼" cubes
•Rinse tomato, chop into ¼" cubes
•Mince garlic into smallest reasonable bits
•Rinse onion, remove top layer, chop into ¼" cubes
•Put all ingredients in a large pot
•Cover with chicken broth
•Put lid on pot and cook on medium for 45 minutes
•Serve in two bowls
•All that's left is for *someone* to kiss the cook

ADVICE FROM A REAL LIVE GIRL:
YOU CAN SUBSTITUTE VEGGIE STOCK FOR THE
CHICKEN STOCK IF YOUR DATE IS VEGETARIAN. THIS
DISH WILL STILL BE
DELICIOUS AND HEARTY.

NOT A MISS STEAK

I'D STEAK MY REPUTATION ON IT

> *NOT EVERYONE KNOWS THIS,*
> *BUT STEAK IS A CUT ABOVE OTHER BITS OF MEAT*

2 steaks, ½ lb each
Olive oil : 1 tbsp for steaks and 1 tbsp for pan
salt & pepper

For the sauce:
4 tbsp butter
1 cup red wine
½ cup beef broth

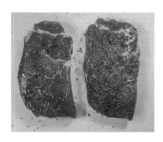

•Coat steaks with olive oil
•Sprinkle salt & pepper on both sides
•Let steaks reach room temperature (20 minutes)
•Get out a 12" skillet and add 1 tbsp olive oil
•Heat on medium until hot, 1-2 minutes
•Place steaks in pan for 5-7 minutes each side
•Move steaks to a plate to cool
•Leave drippings in the pan, turn heat to low
•Melt 4 tbsp butter in skillet
•Add red wine and broth
•Cook, stirring constantly for 5 minutes until thick
•Put sauce in a little ramekin/bowl
•Serve with a side dish of your choice
•All that's left is for *someone* to kiss the cook

ADVICE FROM A REAL LIVE GIRL:
IN LIEU OF THE RED WINE+BROTH, YOU CAN
MARINATE IN CHUCKMAN'S ALL PURPOSE
MARINADE, PAGE 124,
AND USE IT AS THE COOKING SAUCE.

BROCCOLI IN AWESOME SAUCE

THE SECRET INGREDIENT IS AWESOMENESS

NOT EVERYONE KNOWS THIS, BUT MANY QUARTERBACKS TRY TO AVOID EATING THE BROCCOLI, FOR FEAR IT MIGHT "ROUGHAGE THE PASSER"

2 broccoli crowns (softball sized)
8 oz can sliced water chestnuts
3 tbsp olive oil
4 tbsp soy sauce
1 tbsp hot chili sauce
1 cup rice (uncooked)

- Combine rice and 2 cups water in 8" pot
- Bring to a boil, then reduce heat to low/simmer
- Cover with lid, cook 15-20 minutes until rice is done
- Rinse broccoli, chop crowns into ½" morsels
- Drain water chestnuts
- Put 3 tbsp oil in 12" pan, turn burner to medium high
- After 1 minute, add broccoli and stir to coat with oil

- Cover with lid for 3 minutes to steam broccoli
- Add water chestnuts, chili sauce, soy sauce, and vinegar
- Stir to coat and cover for 2 minutes
- Stir, cooking for 2-3 more minutes without lid
- All that's left is for *someone* to kiss the cook

DELICIOUS FISH

A VAST IMPROVEMENT ON SKETCHY FISH

NOT EVERYONE KNOWS THIS, BUT FISH ARE EXCELLENT AT DATA ENTRY; GIVE THEM ANY APPLICATION AND THEY'LL FILLET RIGHT OUT

(2) ½ lb each halibut fillets (or fish of your preference)

1 lemon

1 pint cherry tomatoes

1 bunch/lb asparagus

1 lemon

3 tbsp olive oil

salt & pepper

aluminum foil

- Preheat oven to 350°F
- Place an 18" section of foil on a baking sheet
- Pour 1 tbsp olive oil in the middle
- Place the fish on the olive oil
- Sprinkle with salt and pepper
- Rinse tomatoes, cut each in half, place on fish
- Rinse asparagus, cut off 2" stem bottom (discard)
- Place asparagus on top of the fish
- Pour 2 tbsp olive oil over vegetables
- Slice lemon to ¼" thick rounds
- Place on top of the fish
- Sprinkle with salt and pepper
- Fold foil around ingredients so it won't leak
- Bake 30 minutes until fish is done & veggies tender
- Remove from oven and allow foil to cool 5 minutes
- All that's left is for *someone* to kiss the cook

ANECDOTE FROM A REAL LIVE GIRL:
THIS DISH IS ONE OF THE FIRST ENTREES THE
CHUCKMAN LEARNED TO COOK FOR THE LADIES.
IT HOLDS A SPECIAL PLACE IN OUR HEARTS.

AN EMOTIONAL MESS

QUINOA IS A SUPER FOOD, AND THIS IS A SUPER MEAL, SHOW HER YOU'RE A SUPER GUY

● ●

NOT EVERYONE KNOWS THIS, BUT SOME WOMEN ARE EMOTIONAL: DON'T BELIEVE ME? SOME WOMEN READING THIS JUST GOT ANGRY AT THAT STATEMENT.

1 cup quinoa

1 tsp salt

6 oz tomato paste from a can

2 tbsp apple cider vinegar

1 tsp mustard seed

1 chipotle chili in adobo sauce

¼ cup honey

⅛ tsp cayenne pepper

2 tbsp water

¼ yellow onion

hamburger buns

•Combine quinoa, salt, and water in an 8" pot

•Cover and bring to a boil on medium high

•Simmer on medium-low for 20 minutes then turn off

•Mince onion as finely as possible

•Chop adobo chili as finely as possible

•Combine tomato paste, vinegar, spices, water, and honey in a 8" bowl

 •Add onion, pepper, and all spices to make BBQ sauce

•When quinoa is done, stir in BBQ sauce

•Heat for an additional 5 minutes

•Toast buns and serve sloppy joe style

•All that's left is for *someone* to kiss the cook

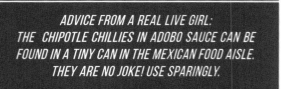

ADVICE FROM A REAL LIVE GIRL:
THE CHIPOTLE CHILLIES IN ADOBO SAUCE CAN BE
FOUND IN A TINY CAN IN THE MEXICAN FOOD AISLE.
THEY ARE NO JOKE! USE SPARINGLY.

MAN, IT'S CHILI IN HERE

MAN IN A CAN

NOT EVERYONE KNOWS THIS, BUT CHILI WAS ORIGINALLY INVENTED BY EARLY SKETCHY TRAVELING CIRCUS FOLK, WHICH IS WHY EVEN TO THIS DAY IT'S POPULARLY REFERRED TO AS "CHILI CON CARNE"

1 lb ground beef
1 tbsp olive oil
½ yellow onion
16 oz canned tomato soup
16 oz canned diced tomatoes
16 oz canned kidney beans
8 oz canned corn
1 green bell pepper
2 tbsp chili powder
1 tsp salt

For topping:
grated cheese
sour cream

•Put beef in a 12" skillet
•Cook on medium until browned
•Rinse onion, remove top layer, chop into ¼"
 cubes
•Drain and rinse corn and beans
•Rinse bell pepper and chop into ¼" cubes
•Get out a 9" pot
•Put browned beef, all canned vegetables, and
spices in pot
•Cover and simmer on low heat for 1 hour
•Pour into a serving bowl
•Top with shredded cheese and sour cream
•All that's left is for *someone* to kiss the cook

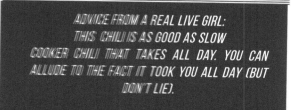

ADVICE FROM A REAL LIVE GIRL:
THIS CHILI IS AS GOOD AS SLOW
COOKER CHILI THAT TAKES ALL DAY. YOU CAN
ALLUDE TO THE FACT IT TOOK YOU ALL DAY (BUT
DON'T LIE).

WILD RICE SLAMMIN' SALMON

IT'S LIKE AN EDIBLE PINK POLO SHIRT

NOT EVERYONE KNOWS THIS, BUT IF YOU REGARD ANY KIND OF RICE AS "WILD", YOU DON'T GET OUT ENOUGH

(2) ½lb fresh salmon fillets
1 lemon
¼ tsp salt
¼ tsp pepper
1 tbsp olive oil
1 tbsp butter
½ tsp dried dill
¾ cup dry wild rice
1 ½ cups water
tin foil

- Preheat oven to 350°F
- Place 24" of tinfoil over an oven-safe baking sheet
- Spread 1 tbsp olive oil in the middle of the foil
- Place the salmon skin-down on the olive oil
- Squeeze the juice out of the lemon over the fish
- Place lemon halves next to the fish on the foil
- Divide butter in half, one piece on each fillet
- Sprinkle the fish with salt, pepper, and dill
- Fold the foil around fish, creating leak-proof packet
- Bake 40 minutes, until fish is cooked and flaky
- While fish bakes, boil 1 ½ cups water in an 8" pot
- Add dry wild rice to boiling water
- Cover and reduce to medium heat so still boiling
- Boil 25 minutes until rice is cooked
- Divide rice and salmon onto two plates
- Drizzle juices collected in the packet over fish
- All that's left is for *someone* to kiss the cook

ADVICE FROM A REAL LIVE GIRL:
SALMON FILLETS SOMETIMES HAVE LITTLE PIN BONES IN THEM. IF YOU SEE THEM, PULL THEM OUT PRIOR TO COOKING. AND WARN YOUR DATE ABOUT THEM.

ODE TO THE LUNCH LADY

THE NATIONAL FOOD OF LUNCH LADIES, AND FRIDAYS EVERYWHERE

*NOT EVERYONE KNOWS THIS,
BUT SOUP IS TO SANDWICH AS MILK IS TO COOKIE*

15 oz canned tomato soup
4 slices of bread
sliced cheddar cheese
2 tbsp butter

•Before the lady arrives, open soup, pour into pot
•Recycle the can
•You can toss extra fresh ingredients in too... like basil! cheese! sour cream!
•Cut 2 tbsp butter into 4 pieces
•Spread one piece butter on each piece of bread
•Place two pieces of bread, butter down, on large skillet
•Put a layer of cheese on each piece of bread
•Top with two more pieces of bread, butter up
•Grill until lightly brown, about 4 minutes each side
•Serve a little bowl of soup next to each sammich
•All that's left is for *someone* to kiss the cook

ADVICE FROM A REAL LIVE GIRL:
READ THE SOUP CAN AND SEE IF IT'S THE KIND
WHERE YOU HAVE TO ADD WATER.

SQUASH IT

NOT EVERYONE KNOWS THIS, BUT SOME FEMALE VEGETABLES ARE INEXPLICABLY LESS VALUED/COVETED BY CERTAIN CHEFS; A PHENOMENON KNOWN AS THE "GLASS CILANTRO"

1 cup rice
2 cups water
1 tbsp olive oil
½ yellow onion
½ lb butternut squash
1 cup green peas
3 tbsp peanut oil
1 tsp coriander
1 tsp cumin
4 tbsp cilantro
15 oz can coconut milk
2/3 cup cashews

•Combine rice and 2 cups water in 8" pot
•Bring to a boil on high, then reduce to simmer
•Cover with a lid and cook 15 minutes to absorb
•Rinse, peel, seed, and ½" cube butternut squash
•Rinse cilantro, remove stems, and mince leaves
•Put oil, onions, cumin, and coriander in 12" skillet
•Cook 5 minutes until onions are clear
•Add the squash and stir fry for 5 minutes
•Add the coconut milk, peas, and cashews
•Turn heat to low, cover, cook for 30 minutes
•Garnish with cilantro
•Serve over rice
•All that's left is for *someone* to kiss the cook

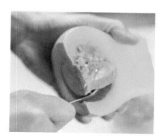

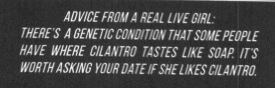

ADVICE FROM A REAL LIVE GIRL:
THERE'S A GENETIC CONDITION THAT SOME PEOPLE
HAVE WHERE CILANTRO TASTES LIKE SOAP. IT'S
WORTH ASKING YOUR DATE IF SHE LIKES CILANTRO.

SPAGHETTPEAS

YOU'RE GOING TO GIVE CARBOHYDRATES A COMPLEX

NOT EVERYONE KNOWS THIS, BUT THE PEA IS MOTHER NATURE'S TINY, GREEN, VEGETARIAN MEATBALL

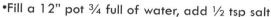

4 tbsp butter

4 oz prosciutto

½ small yellow onion

½ red pepper

1 cup peas

1 bunch parsley

1 lb dry spaghetti pasta

•Fill a 12" pot ¾ full of water, add ½ tsp salt
•Bring water to a boil on high, reduce to medium
•Add pasta and cook per package directions
•Drain pasta and pour into a large bowl
•Rinse onion, remove top layer, chop into ¼"
  pieces

•Rinse pepper, remove stems and seeds, chop
  into ¼" pieces
•Chop prosciutto into ½" pieces
•Rinse parsley, remove stems, mince leaves
•In a 10" skillet melt butter over medium heat
•Add prosciutto, parsley, salt, pepper, and onion,
  cook until onion is clear

•Add peas and cook for 5 more minutes
•Pour prosciutto/peas mixture over pasta, stir to
  combine
•All that's left is for *someone* to kiss the cook

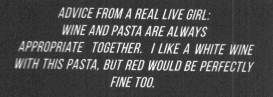

*ADVICE FROM A REAL LIVE GIRL:
WINE AND PASTA ARE ALWAYS
APPROPRIATE TOGETHER. I LIKE A WHITE WINE
WITH THIS PASTA, BUT RED WOULD BE PERFECTLY
FINE TOO.*

PASTAFARIAN

WE BE GLUT'EN MON

NOT EVERYONE KNOWS THIS, BUT PASTA IS JAMAICA'S THIRTEENTH MOST POPULAR MUNCHIE

½ lb dry spaghetti
1 tbsp olive oil
1 clove garlic
5 Roma tomatoes
½ yellow onion
3 tbsp fresh basil
1 tsp oregano
½ tsp salt
3 tbsp tomato paste
½ cup grated parmesan cheese

•Bring a 10" pot of water to a boil
•Add noodles, cook per directions on package
•Usually takes 8 minutes, cook until tender
•Drain pasta and pour into serving bowl
•Rinse onion, remove top layer, chop into ⅛"
 pieces
•Rinse tomato, chop into ¼" pieces
•Rinse basil, remove stems, and mince leaves
•Mince garlic into smallest reasonable pieces
•Combine oil, tomatoes, onion, and garlic in a 10"
 skillet
•Bring to boil on medium high, then cook 5
 minutes
•Stir slowly but constantly to prevent scorching
•Stir in basil, oregano, and tomato paste, cook 1
 more minute
•Pour tomato sauce over noodles
•Top with cheese
•All that's left is for *someone* to kiss the cook

ADVICE FROM A REAL LIVE GIRL:
IF YOU GRAB A SPAGHETTI NOODLE AND THROW IT
AT THE WALL AND ITS STICKS,
IT'S DONE!

FETTUCCINE OF THE FRED...O

I'M NOT ALFREDO COMMITMENT!

NOT EVERYONE KNOWS THIS, BUT FETTUCCINE ALFREDO ORIGINATED IN ITALY...
SURE, MOST PEOPLE KNOW IT, BUT NOT EVERYONE...

½ lb dry fettuccine noodles

1 stick butter (½ cup)

1 tsp garlic

1 cup heavy cream

2 cups grated parmesan cheese

1 tsp salt

1 tsp pepper

1 tsp oregano

- Fill a 12" pot ¾ full with water and bring to a boil
- Add fettuccine, cook per package instructions
- Drain pasta and pour into large serving bowl
- Cover with a plate or foil to keep it hot
- Mince garlic into smallest reasonable pieces
- Combine butter, garlic, salt, pepper, and oregano in a 12" skillet
- Cook on medium until butter melts, reduce to low
- Add cream and parmesean
- Cook for 5 minutes, stirring constantly
- Pour cream mixture over pasta and toss to combine
- All that's left is for *someone* to kiss the cook

ADVICE FROM A REAL LIVE GIRL:
DON'T TURN THE HEAT UP TO COOK THIS FASTER,
THE CREAM WILL SCORCH.

LASAGMA

JUST LIKE MA' USED TO MAKE

NOT EVERYONE KNOWS THIS, BUT LASAGNA SHOULD BE ENJOYED WITH
AN EXCESS OF RED WINE, AS SHOULD ALL ITALIAN FOOD... AND ALL
OTHER KINDS OF FOOD

1 lb ground Italian sausage	2 tbsp olive oil
16 oz jar tomato sauce	1 tsp garlic
1 box no-cook lasagna noodles	2 tsp basil
2 cups ricotta cheese	2 tsp oregano
1 cup parmesan cheese	½ tsp salt
1 cup mozzarella for cheese mixture	½ tsp pepper
½ cup mozzarella cheese for topping	tin foil

- Preheat oven to 375°F
- Mince garlic into smallest reasonable pieces
- Rinse basil, remove stems, and mince leaves
- Put sausage, oil, garlic, basil, and oregano in a 12" skillet
- Cook on medium 8 minutes, stirring occasionally
- Add tomato sauce, stir
- Cook on medium for 10 minutes
    - This is now your meat sauce

- In a separate bowl, combine ricotta, parmesan, and 1 cup mozzarella
- Stir to combine while sprinkling in salt and pepper
    - This is now your cheese mixture.
- Spray a 4 quart oven safe baking dish with olive oil
- Layer items in the pan in the following order:
    - noodles on bottom
    - meat sauce
    - cheese mixture
    - noodles again
    - meat sauce again
    - cheese mixture again
    - noodles on top

- Sprinkle remaining ½ cup of mozzarella on top
- Cover with tin foil and bake for 45 minutes
- Cool for 5 minutes after removing from the oven
- Cut into pieces and serve
- All that's left is for *someone* to kiss the cook

PAD SE EW, SAY ME

PAD SE EW, EW GOT WHAT I NEED

NOT EVERYONE KNOWS THIS, BUT IN A RECENT UNOFFICIAL POLL PAD SE EW AND FRIED RICE RECEIVED THE EXACT SAME NUMBER OF VOTES FOR BEST FOOD EVER;
IT WAS A THAI

3 ½ oz dry rice noodles

1 tbsp chili oil

1 tsp garlic

½ white onion

1 tbsp hot chili sauce

2 cups broccoli crowns

4 tbsp soy sauce

2 eggs

- Cook noodles per package directions
- Drain noodles well once cooked
- Heat oil on medium-high in wok or large skillet
- Mince garlic into smallest reasonable pieces
- Rinse onion, remove top layer, chop into ¼" cubes
- Rinse broccoli, chop crowns into ½" morsels
- Add onion and garlic, cook until onion is clear
- Add broccoli and hot chili sauce, cook 3 minutes
- Pour noodles and soy sauce on top, stir to coat
- Use spatula to push noodles to sides
- Crack eggs into the clear spot, scrambling
- When eggs are cooked stir to mix in with noodles
- All that's left is for *someone* to kiss the cook

ADVICE FROM A REAL LIVE GIRL:
THIS DISH IS VERY SIMILAR TO THE
CLASSIC FAVORITE: PAD THAI

THE 'LEEKY' WOK

TAKE A WOK ON THE WILD SIDE-DISH

3 large carrots
1 stalk leeks
2 oranges
2 tbsp ketchup
1 tbsp honey
2 tbsp soy sauce
2 tbsp olive oil
½ cup peanuts

•Rinse carrots, grate with cheese grater
•Cut white stalk off of leek, discard
•Separate green leaves and individually rinse
•Cut into ¼" wide, 4" long, bite-size strips
•Peel orange, remove seeds, chop into ½" cubes
•Pour oil in 12" skillet, heat on high for 2 minutes
•Add carrots and leeks, cook 5 minutes until soft
•Add orange pieces and cook for 3 more minutes
•In a small bowl, mix ketchup, honey, and soy
 sauce
•Add ketchup mixture and peanuts, cook 2
 minutes
•Poor out onto a serving plate/platter
•All that's left is for *someone* to kiss the cook

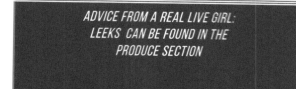

ADVICE FROM A REAL LIVE GIRL:
LEEKS CAN BE FOUND IN THE
PRODUCE SECTION

SNOW PEAS STIR FRYING THE COOP

WINTER IS COMING; AND IT'S DELICIOUS

NOT EVERYONE KNOWS THIS, BUT A LOT OF SERIOUS CONTROVERSY IS GOING ON IN THE COOKING VERSE ABOUT WOK FRIED FOODS, BUT WE DON'T WANT TO STIR THE POT

2 tbsp olive oil

1 tsp chili flakes

½ yellow onion

1 lb chicken breast

4 tbsp hoisin sauce

6 oz snow peas, or one package

1 red bell pepper

1 cup cashews

1 cup dry rice

- Combine rice and 2 cups water in 8" pot
- Bring to a boil on high, then reduce to simmer/ low
- Cover with a lid and cook 15 minutes to absorb
- Rinse onion, remove top layer, chop into ¼" cubes
- Rinse chicken, remove any excess fat, and cut into 1" bite size pieces
- Rinse red pepper, remove stem/seeds, chop into ¼" cubes
- In a 12" skillet combine olive oil and chili flakes
- Cook on medium heat for 1 minute
- Add onion and cook until it's clear, about 8 minutes
- Add chicken and Hoisin sauce to skillet
- Cook for 8 minutes until chicken is done, stirring
- Add snow peas, bell pepper, and cashews
- Cook for 5 minutes
- Divide the rice on two plates
- Top with stir fry
- All that's left is for *someone* to kiss the cook

ADVICE FROM A REAL LIVE GIRL:
HOISIN SAUCE IS MAGIC. IT CAN BE FOUND IN THE
ASIAN FOOD AISLE IN A BOTTLE.

RICE WITH STUFF IN IT

HOPEFULLY SHE'S INTO STUFF

*NOT EVERYONE KNOWS THIS, BUT YESTERDAY'S OLD STALE RICE IS
TODAY'S FRESH DELICIOUS FRIED RICE
(AFTER YOU FRY IT AND ADD FRESH STUFF)*

2 cups cold cooked rice

1 tsp chili flakes

2 tbsp olive oil

1 bunch/lb asparagus

½ yellow onion

1 carrot

1 cup green peas

2 cups spinach

1 tbsp soy sauce

2 eggs

- Rinse asparagus, cut/discard bottom 2" of stem
- Cut remaining asparagus into 1" lengths
- Rinse onion, remove outer layer, chop into ¼" pieces
- Rinse carrot, chop into ⅛" discs
- Rinse spinach, remove and discard stems
- Combine olive oil and chili flakes in 12" skillet
- Heat on medium for one minute
- Add the onion and cook until clear
- Add asparagus, carrots, spinach, and peas
- Cook for 5 minutes
- Add the cold rice and soy sauce
- Cook for 5 minutes or until rice is hot
- Use spatula to push rice to sides
- Crack the eggs into the clear spot, scrambling
- Once egg is cooked stir to mix egg & rice together
- All that's left is for *someone* to kiss the cook

ADVICE FROM A REAL LIVE GIRL:
BE A HERO: PRE-COOK THE RICE EARLY IN THE DAY
AND LET IT COOL. IF YOU'RE A FAN OF SHRIMP FRIED
RICE, GET A 12 OZ PACKAGE OF FROZEN COOKED
SHRIMP AND THROW IT IN THE SKILLET WHEN YOU
PUT IN THE VEGETABLES.

'DON'T EVEN NEED A RECIPE' CHICKEN TACOS

DON'T BE PALTRY WITH THE POULTRY

*NOT EVERYONE KNOWS THIS,
BUT YOU DO NEED A RECIPE, OTHERWISE IT'S JUST STUFF*

Meat Filling:
1 lb ground chicken
½ white onion
1 packet taco seasoning
1 lb ground chicken
1 bag of tortillas
olive oil

Taco Bar Toppings:
>sliced black olives
>guacamole
>salsa
>grated cheese
>sour cream

•Wrap tortillas in foil, heat in oven at 200°F while meat cooks
•Rinse onion, remove top layer, chop into ¼" pieces
•Put oil, onion, and seasoning, in 12" skillet
•Cook on medium for 5 minutes
•Add chicken, stir to break into bite sized morsels
•Cook until no pink is left inside any morsel
•Set taco bar toppings out on little bowls or plates
•Allow guest to customize her taco to her liking
•All that's left is for *someone* to kiss the cook

ADVICE FROM A REAL LIVE GIRL:
IF YOU'RE FEELING FRISKY, MAKE YOUR OWN
GUACAMOLE AND SALSA FOR THE TACO BAR. SEE
PAGES 134 AND 128 FOR RECIPES.

A MEXICAN HOT TUB

NOW WE'RE TOC'IN

NOT EVERYONE KNOWS THIS, BUT IF YOU SERVE MEXICAN FOOD LEFTOVERS WARMED UP THE FOLLOWING DAY YOU CAN MAKE THEM SOUND MORE APPETIZING BY CALLING IT "REFAJITED"

*slow cooker

(This recipe takes all day)

Soup:

1 lb ground beef

16 oz can red kidney beans

16 oz can black beans

16 oz can tomato sauce

16 oz water

16 oz canned corn

1 packet taco seasoning mix

1 packet ranch dressing mix

Taco Bar:

sliced black olives

guacamole

salsa

1 bag corn chips

grated cheese

sour cream

•Drain kidney beans, black beans, and corn
•Add all soup ingredients except meat to slow cooker
•Brown ground beef on medium in 12" skillet
•Drain grease into empty, melt-proof can
•Add meat to slow cooker
•Stir once, cover, and cook on low 7-8 hours
•The longer it cooks the better
•Serve with hearty corn chips and taco bar toppings
•All that's left is for *someone* to kiss the cook

ADVICE FROM A REAL LIVE GIRL:
IF YOU DON'T HAVE A SLOW COOKER, USE A BIG POT
ON THE STOVE AND COOK ON MEDIUM-LOW FOR 45
MINUTES.

SNACKHACKS

• •

> Some food components, or "snacks" if you will, are so literally self-explanatory (the directions are simple and right on the box) that they don't warrant a recipe; however, it's a useful resource to have a list of options/ideas to choose from:

(The below are all available at the Butcher counter already fully prepared)

Beef Short Ribs
Teriyaki Flank Steaks
Herb Chicken Kabob
Herb Beef Kabob
Lemon Chicken Kabob
Marinated Chicken
Black Pepper Chicken
Turkey Burgers
Fresh Sausage
Fresh Bacon
Bacon Wrapped Fillets
Brat wurst
Italian Sausage
Pork Tenderloins
Fajita Seasoned Beef
Teriyaki Flank Steak
Stuffed Chicken Breasts
Kabobs
Southwest Chicken Breasts
Apple Almond Chicken Breasts
BBQ Pork
Popcorn Chicken

Salmon Patties
Crab Cakes
Seafood Salad
Seafood Spread
Shrimp Cocktail Tray
Smoked Salmon
Fresh Breaded Fish
Fresh Marinated Fish
Fresh Rubbed Fish
Cod Dijon
Tuna Steaks
Smoked Alaskan Scallops
Crab
Candied Salmon
Cooked Shrimp
Swordfish Steaks
Tempura Shrimp
Cedar Planked Salmon
Popcorn Shrimp
Crab & Shrimp Seafood Feast
Salmon Burgers

CHAPTER 3

DESSERT

Dessert finally provides a long overdue food based reward for the hard work of eating all that other food throughout the day. Dessert dares to ask the question, "should I have multiple complementary dishes served successively for this meal," and answers: "of course."

CRISPLESS APPLE CRISPS
THIS WILL HELP HER FIND YOU "APPEALING"

NOT EVERYONE KNOWS THIS, BUT APPARENTLY THE APPLES IN THE STATE OF WASHINGTON ARE BIGGER THAN THE APPLES ONE FINDS ELSEWHERE...WE'RE #1 :P

2 apples (any)
1 tsp cinnamon
¼ cup brown sugar
1 lemon

- Preheat oven to 350°F
- Rinse, peel, and halve apples, remove stems/ seeds (seeds can be removed with a spoon)
- Put apples in a bowl and squeeze lemon over them
- Sprinkle apples with sugar and cinnamon
- Stir apples around in the bowl with a spatula
- Place them in the baking dish flat side down
- Cover the baking dish with foil
- Bake for 20 minutes, or until apples are tender
- Allow to cool
- All that's left is for *someone* to kiss the cook

ADVICE FROM A REAL LIVE GIRL:
THIS DISH MAKES THE HOUSE SMELL AMAZING. IF YOU CAN, PREP THESE APPLES IN THE PAN BEFORE YOUR DATE ARRIVES AND PUT THEM IN THE OVEN WHEN YOU SIT DOWN TO EAT DINNER. BONUS POINTS FOR SERVING WITH VANILLA ICE CREAM.

THE LAST STRAWBERRIES

SKINNY DIPPIN'

NOT EVERYONE KNOWS THIS, BUT JUST ABOUT ANY FRUIT IS MORE ENJOYABLE DIPPED IN A SUFFICIENT AMOUNT OF MELTED CHOCOLATE

½ lb semi-sweet chocolate candy bark (the kind in the microwaveable tray)
1 pint strawberries
wax paper

•Rinse strawberries and place on a paper towel to dry
•Microwave the chocolate per package directions
•Holding the stem, dip strawberry in chocolate
•Place each on wax paper to cool
•All that's left is for *someone* to kiss the cook

ADVICE FROM A REAL LIVE GIRL:
BEST NOT TO BUST THESE OUT ON THE FIRST DATE.
THEY ARE MORE OF A THIRD DATE KIND OF FOOD.
CHOCOLATE BARK MAY BE FOUND IN THE BAKING
AISLE.

EASY, BREEZY BROWNIES
SHOW HER THAT YOU'LL NEVER DESSERT HER LOVE

NOT EVERYONE KNOWS THIS, BUT BROWNIES CAN BE LEFT TO COOL, THEY DON'T HAVE TO BE EATEN IMMEDIATELY AND IN THEIR ENTIRETY WHILE STILL WARM

1 box brownie mix
1 bag semi-sweet chocolate chips
eggs
vegetable oil
water

•Preheat oven to setting listed on box
•Follow the instructions on the box to make batter
•Add chocolate chips
•Spray a baking dish with nonstick oil spray
•Pour batter into greased baking dish
•Bake according to the instructions on the box
•All that's left is for *someone* to kiss the cook

ADVICE FROM A REAL LIVE GIRL:
ADDING THE CHOCOLATE CHIPS IS A NICE TOUCH
HERE. BE SURE TO THROW AWAY THE BOX AFTER
READING THE DIRECTIONS SO SHE WILL THINK
YOU MADE THE BROWNIES FROM SCRATCH.

NICE CREAM

IT TAKES TWO SPOONS TO SPOON...*MIND BLOWN*

NOT EVERYONE KNOWS THIS, BUT PUTTING FRENCH VANILLA ICE CREAM IN A PORTER OR A CHOCOLATE STOUT IS BEERILLIANT

1 container (her favorite) ice cream

*hint: buy the good/expensive stuff

•Scoop ice cream into bowls
•Bonus points: One bowl with two spoons
•All that's left is for *someone* to kiss the cook

(CHOCOLATE) BAR WITH ME

DARKNESS CACAOUNTS

NOT EVERYONE KNOWS THIS, BUT CHOCOLATE IS THE NUMBER ONE FOOD CRAVED BY AMERICAN WOMEN AND RELEASES ENDORPHINS IN THEIR BRAINS SIMILAR TO LOVE

1 bar of dark chocolate (85% cacao or greater)

•Buy some fancy-schmancy dark chocolate
 •The higher the Cacao % the better
 •Red wine also dude, red wine
•All that's left is for *someone* to kiss the cook

**ADVICE FROM A REAL LIVE GIRL:
DUDE. RED WINE.**

SNACKHACKS

• •

Some food components, or "snacks" if you will, are so literally self-explanatory (the directions are simple and right on the box) that they don't warrant a recipe; however, it's a useful resource to have a list of options/ideas to choose from:

(The below are all available in the Bakery already fully prepared)

Apple strudel
Baklava
Berliner
Cake
Cannoli
Cookies
Cream horn
Cream puff
Cronut
Cupcake
Danish
Donuts
Éclair
Macaroons
Nun's puffs
Pie
Pudding
Streusel
Strudel
Tarts
Tortes
Turnovers

ACKNOWLEDGEMENTS

The writers of this book would like to thank all our friends and family who helped with this book through Kickstarter, recipes, encouragement, and by saying "oh yeah, I know someone who NEEDS that book" all along the way.

An especially thankful thanks belongs to Noah Kassos, a.k.a. "Tachomie", a.k.a @noahkassos on Instagram. This was not your passion project, it was ours, and we are grateful that your passion for Christy Beaver, and help finishing the snacks we produced, was fuel enough to sacrifice many a weekend photographing for us.

To Dillon Webster for the graphic design work, you are truly of or related to the pictorial arts, sir.

To Rosalie Schlenk, for cleaning up the final manuscript so well it's like Charles and The Beav had nothing to do with the project at all.

To Art Castelleja whose supportive exuberance was exceeded only by his access to elaborate kitchen settings.

To June Dunn and Mamaw Beaver, without whom Christy may never have learned to meet every culinary challenge, and be able to share a fraction of her wealth of culinary knowledge with Charles, and men everywhere.

To Charles' Tiny Momma, who cooked so excellently it never occurred to Charles that maybe he should learn to cook for himself. And to his father, who also never cooked (see above about Tiny Momma.)

ABOUT THE AUTHORS

CHRISTY BEAVER was raised in Southern Arkansas, where she began learning from her mother and grandmother in the kitchen as soon as she could walk. Like any good Southern lady, she developed a lifelong love of comfort food and sharing food with others.

Christy is an unintentional collector of complexly-emotioned creatures including her curmudgeonly devoted dachshund, Andy, and her curmudgeonier devoted friend (and co-author), The Chuckman.

Upon learning of Charles' ineptitude in the kitchen, as well as with the ladies, Christy handcrafted a gift for him that resulted in the prototype for this cookbook; "Chuckman's Book of Recipes to Impress the Ladies."

Christy now resides in Seattle, where she has published three cookbooks and continues to help Charles, and now hopefully men everywhere, to considerately and tastefully cook for the ladies in their lives.

CHARLES LIOTTA, a self-declared "punthusiast", resides in Seattle where he actively pursues his two great passions; avoiding people, and not-doing-stuff.

Charles grew up in pastoral rural eastern Washington (GO COUGS!!!) the last of 19 children, and goes by "Uncle the Chuckman" to his 70+ nieces and nephews.

Charles has developed a well-beyond-healthy fear of the fairer sex, so of course it stood to reason he should endeavour to co-author a book about the two things he understands the least in this world, cooking and women.

Charles hopes to one day open a full-scale catering business that expanded from a confectionery; its name will be "Revenge." It's motto will be: "Revenge: It's not 'just desserts' anymore."

PLACE TAKE OUT MENUS HERE
IN CASE IT ALL GOES AWRY.

Made in the USA
Lexington, KY
26 February 2017